COLONIAL VILLAGE

Kittery Point, Maine

By

John Eldridge Frost

Published by the
KITTERY HISTORICAL AND NAVAL SOCIETY
Kittery, Maine
2021

Kittery Historical and Naval Society
P.O. Box 453
Kittery, ME 03904

kitterymuseum.com

Printed in the United States of America

Colonial Village

1647-1947

Kittery Point, Maine

A study of the changes that have taken place in certain typical
buildings of a three hundred year old village.

INTRODUCTION

The purpose of this study is two-fold:

(1) to illustrate the forces that make ancient buildings of great interest, and

(2) to portray the life that centers about the buildings of an American colonial village throughout its history.

For this study, I have selected a village with buildings that represent varied architectural types, or buildings that were designed to fulfill particular functions.

The greater number of American colonial villages that have survived the ravages of fire, decay, and "improvement" appear to us only in part. To locate a village possessing a representative collection of colonial buildings of more than average significance, it has been necessary to select one on the seacoast where the lanes of commerce with Europe and the European colonial empires led to American doors.

Since colonial times, Kittery Point village has seen a number of changes. Yet many of the old buildings seem to nod across the street to one another like old friends. Furthermore, they seem to tolerate with a natural dignity the growth of new buildings among them. Many of the old buildings once sat in far-stretching acres and are now confined to small gardens. They have lost none of their graciousness and charm by the alteration of circumstances, but seem to profit by contrast with the architecture of post-colonial years. If it appears that post-colonial houses of Kittery Point are much neglected in this study, I hasten to add that the neglect was intentional. The relationship that the old buildings bear to one another is much stronger than the relationship they bear to the buildings that have followed.

These old buildings are monuments of history. The life that has been lived within them typifies the life that has passed in many American buildings that are colonial survivals. This life is worth recording for it illustrates the forces that vitalize historic buildings. To make an objective record of this life, the historian must tell not only of the people who have gained fame and prestige in the world beyond the village, but of those who have led simple lives within the village confines. He must tell not only of those who have done much to preserve the colonial heritage but also of those who have done much to mutilate it.

When any tradition makes a valuable contribution, I have recorded the tradition, and the source of it so far as known. It has been of interest to note how often what had been regarded as tradition was found upon investigation to have a basis of fact.

In gathering material about Kittery Point village, and in compiling this material, I am indebted for many kindnesses, in particular to the late Miss Caroline Lewis Gerrish of Follett House, Joseph W. Cutts of Braemere, Kittery Point, Philip Mason Marston, professor of history at the University of New Hampshire, Mrs. Mary Bellamy Safford Wildes of Kittery, Maine, and Miss Dorothy M. Vaughan, librarian of the Public Library, Portsmouth, New Hampshire.

For the photographs used in this book, I am indebted to Douglas Armsden of Kittery, Maine. An effort has been made to show the houses just as they are today. No attempt has been made to disguise electrical fixtures or other additions; the houses appear just as when used by the present occupants. At the time the photographs were taken, some of the Bellamy carving in Sparhawk Hall had been removed for repairs. An interesting feature of the drawing room at Bray House is the painting (hanging above the fireplace) of Fort McClary by G. S. Wasson.

Houses have been referred to by the name of the house, without the article preceding the name, following the English usage prevalent at Kittery Point, except in instances where the American usage is followed by village residents.

Chapter introductions have been included in an attempt to answer some of the many questions arising in connection with the building under discussion.

This work has been accepted as a thesis for the degree of Master of Arts, in the department of history, at the University of New Hampshire.

JOHN ELDRIDGE FROST.

New Smyrna Beach, Florida
28 November, 1947.

THE VILLAGE

The village is an old form of community life. It is found even among primitive peoples. In Europe, the village, at the time it was most common, generally implied association with some nobleman's estate and the tilling of common land by the community. At the time of the decay of this type of life, the village often consisted of scattered buildings without as closely knit a community life as formerly. In America, because of the heavily wooded areas, the village of scattered homesteads became as common as the compact village. Kittery Point is a scattered village; the buildings discussed in this book lie between the old parsonage and Mitchell Garrison, a distance of three and six-tenths miles.

Kittery Point is not an incorporated village; it is a part of the township of Kittery which, according to the Maine historian Williamson, was incorporated in 1647. The town takes its name from the manor of Kittery Court, (the property of A. L. Hine-Haycock, Esq.) located on Kittery Point in Kingsweare, Devon, across the river Dart from the city of Dartmouth. The old manor house is standing and the house and gardens have been restored. The house is thought to have been a priory at one time. From Kingsweare, the Shapleigh family, first settlers and proprietors of Kittery Point, Maine, came to New England. Kingsweare is ten miles below the birthplace of another Kittery Point pioneer, Capt. Francis Champernowne; the Champernowne manor, Dartington Hall, has been restored by the present owner, L. K. Elmhirst, Esq.

THE EARLY HOUSE

Bray House is the oldest dwelling house in the state of Maine. Perhaps an older building, not a dwelling house, is the Old Gaol in York Village, once dated 1653, the year after York, abandoning its status as the city of Gorgeana (held for twelve years), signed the submission act to Puritan Massachusetts.

The Old Gaol is sometimes said to be the oldest public building in America. The late Col. Charles E. Banks, York's historian, presents evidence that leads us to date the Gaol, 1667.

The oldest dwelling house standing in the United States is located in St. Augustine, Florida, and appears to have been standing there as early as 1599. It is built of coquina rock. The oldest dwelling house in New England is the Fairbanks house in Dedham, erected in 1636 of oak timbers brought from England; this house is very likely the oldest frame house in America. Stone was little used as a building material in New England though the Rev. Henry Whitfield, in 1639, built a stone house in Guilford, Connecticut, which stands today.

Bray House is typical of a style of architecture that is a step away from a type used at that time in England. Houses one room wide with a central chimney and steep winding stairs sufficed the needs of the pioneers till the increase of colonial prosperity caused them to double both rooms and chimney.

THE EARLY HOUSE: BRAY HOUSE, 1662

The most pleasing location in Kittery Point was chosen by John Bray, shipwright, of Plymouth, Devon, for the location of his new-world home. Bray House *(see Fig. 1)* has a commanding view of Portsmouth Harbor. Immediately before it stands little Tavistock Island, like a sentinel to the harbor. Beyond Tavistock the swift flowing Piscataqua River meets the sea. The waves of the Atlantic break upon one side of Tavistock while the waters of the Piscataqua eddy and swirl about the other side of this little island, crowned by one building—a picturesque fishing shack. To the left of Tavistock lies Gunnison's Island[1] which has been owned by the Gunnisons since about 1651, when Hugh Gunnison sold the King's Arms Tavern in Boston and moved to Kittery Point. Gerrish Island to the left and New Castle to the right, dwarfing in size any islands hereabout, give ample background to the Bray House view. Surely the choice of John Bray has been much acclaimed by those who have occupied his new world home in later years.

A tradition regarding this house is that one of the rooms (the West Room) of the Bray house in Kittery Point was patterned after a room in the Bray house in England.[2] We have also the story of Henry James' call at Bray House, Kittery Point. James was brought here by his friend William Dean Howells. When James was shown the angel painted in the corner cupboard of the gracious panelled drawing room he remarked that such also were seen in Devonshire.[3]

During the two hundred and seventy-five years since Bray House was built it has been the scene of much hospitality. The present owners, Mrs. David Wasson and Mrs. Nathan Ayer, in 1947 opened this house to the public at the celebration of the three hundredth anniversary of the incorporation of the town of Kittery, Maine. There have been other hostesses who should not be forgotten for they belong to Bray House, just as Bray House once belonged to them. The parish registers of St. Andrew's Church in Plymouth, Devon, reveal the marriage of John Bray to Joan Hooper, and the baptism of their children;[4] perhaps a more thorough search of these registers would give us some clue to the origin of the patrician features that so distinguish their daughter Margery Bray Pepperrell of Bray House. "Fair Margery Bray", with her two sisters and her

---

1 Gunnison's Island is now the property of Ralph Gunnison of Kittery Point.
2 An interesting feature of Bray House is a controversial panel in the drawing room. Painted in oils at an early date, it is thought by some persons to represent Louisbourg, by others to represent Plymouth, England.
3 Richardson, *John Bray House in Kittery, Maine*, p. 712.
4 MS notes of the late Col. Charles E. Banks, Bangor Public Library, Bangor, Maine.

brother spent their childhood here. Kittery Point residents enjoy the occasional visits made by Mrs. Josiah Low of Boston, who with her many-
talented family made Bray House a vital place in the community life.

If John Bray were to return to Kittery Point, he would find his home
altered and yet preserving the spirit of the original house so completely
that there is no lack of harmony in the group of buildings. The center of
the old house is intact; it dominates the group of buildings joined together. The old ell (the lean-to, with its roof sloping almost to the ground)
that John Bray mentioned in his will, was gone long before the recollec-
tion of anyone now living. In its place on the east end of the house, the
Crosbys, in 1916, built a wing which includes a sun porch overlooking
Portsmouth Harbor; to this has been added in 1947 a large double garage
with servants' quarters, connected to the house by a latticed trellis. To the
west end, Mrs. Low added another house[5] joined to the old house by a
long studio room for which John Benson of Kittery painted an appropriate panel of the rolling Atlantic. In this house on the harbor, erected by a
shipwright, there is ample evidence of the closeness of the sea.

There were few colonists in America who had homes in both the old
world and the new at the same time. John Bray's will mentions his home
in old England and his home in New England. Bray House, the New
England home, was divided as a temporary measure to provide for his
unmarried children.[6] The new end (the West end built somewhat later
than the East end where the old kitchen was located) was given to his
widow Joan, who survived John Bray for three years. The central part of
the house was given to John Bray Jr., while "the lean-to and the chamber
over it" and "the east room and as much of the chamber as is over that"
went to young Mary Bray who had not then become the bride of Joseph
Deering.

Bray House has served several purposes in the course of its history.
From Maine Province and Court Records we learn that the place was a
tavern and seat of the local court. Tradition asserts that a private school
was conducted here for a short while.

Bray House, the oldest dwelling house in the state of Maine, has
within the past half-century had a number of occupants. Before that time
it changed hands but once. For one hundred and ninety-one years, it was
the property of the Bray family; for one hundred three years, it was owned
by the Mitchell family. Mary Bray Deering and her husband Joseph lived

---

5 This building was erected by Thomas O. Hoyt (Gilford, N. H., 1818 – Kittery Point, Me. 1902). Hoyt
(who preceded Theodore Keen as the stage-driver from Portsmouth to Kittery Point) kept a general store
in this building.
6 See Drummond, *John Bray of Kittery.*

in Bray House (which was mentioned in Joseph's will in 1720). Eleven years later, their sons Bray, Clement, William and John divided the estate and Bray received Bray House. Lieut. Bray Deering was an officer in the troops raised to take Louisbourg, in 1745, serving there under his cousin Sir William Pepperrell.[7] Bray Deering's only child, Mary, married Capt. John Underwood of Portsmouth (where their descendants still live). The Underwoods sold Bray House to Benjamin Mitchell. It remained in the Mitchell name till Mrs. Sarah Mitchell, in 1904, transferred it to her daughter Mrs. Nickerson of Dennis on Cape Cod.

In 1910, when the Pepperrell Family Association was at its height (under the presidency of the Hon. Everett Pepperrell Wheeler of New York City, a Bray descendant), the association (under the title of the William Pepperrell Realty Company) acquired the house. Although the association had hoped to restore the house, which at this time was dilapidated, they did not have sufficient funds available. A series of tenants occupied the house till it was purchased by the Crosbys.

Raymond Moreau Crosby,[8] a lithographer and illustrator, is now retired and living in Yarmouthport, Massachusetts. The Crosbys kept Bray House as a summer home, with 252 Boylston Street, Boston, as their winter residence. Mr. Crosby painted murals of scenes in Capri on the west room walls but these have since been removed.

The next occupant of Bray House, Mrs. Susan Taber Freshman, a widow of Brooklyn, New York, leased the house from the Crosbys before she purchased it. Mrs. Freshman's sister, Mrs. Richardson, wrote a full account of the restoring of Bray House, a work undertaken by the Crosbys and completed by Mrs. Freshman (later Mrs. Josiah Low). Mrs. Low sold her Kittery Point home to Robert T. Moreland of Adrian, Michigan, who, after three years, sold it when he purchased an old Wentworth house in Portsmouth.

Mrs. Mildred Coes Wasson (a descendant of the Weeks family of Kittery) and her friend Mrs. Nathan Ayer, both of Bangor, purchased Bray House in 1944. Mrs. Wasson,[9] a graduate of Portsmouth, N. H., High School, and widow of David Arnold Wasson (writer and marine expert of Kittery Point) is a novelist, author of several books and stories published in English and American magazines.

---

7 Noyes, *Genealogical Dictionary of Maine and New Hampshire*, p. 191.
8 See *Who's Who in America*, v. 14, 1926-27. Crosby (Grand Rapids, Mich., 1876-   ), a Yale alumnus, studied painting abroad. Crosby's sketches and drawings have been published in the *Saturday Evening Post, Life*, and *Collier's Weekly*. In recent years R. M. Crosby has specialized in portraits. Mrs. Crosby was the daughter of the Rev. Charles Gordon Ames of Boston.
9 See *Who's Who in America*, v. 24, 1946-47, p. 2884. She is a daughter-in-law of the late G. S. Wasson mentioned elsewhere in this book.

The evolution of Bray House to its present state is reminiscent of the evolution of some of the great English country houses where each generation has added whatever was necessary to meet the changing ways of living without removing what had been used by previous generations. The oldest part of Bray House is furnished in antique furniture. The house was one room wide, so the rooms are light and airy. John Bray's kitchen has become a dining room while the old parlor is now the drawing room. The building remains functional as it was originally intended to be. A single chimney pierces the center of the house and the steep narrow stairs, typical of the early American house, rise abruptly to Mistress Bray's bedrooms overhead.

THE GREAT HOUSE

If chronological sequence were followed in this work, the great house would appear at the close of the discussion of village architecture. For contrast, however, we can see the great house more clearly when it is next to the early house. The early house was utilitarian, the great house was built for display. It reflected the prosperity of the owner.

The great house was the forerunner of the Federal house which it closely resembled. Instead of being distinctly oblong in shape, like most of its contemporaries, it more nearly approached the square. Lavish in proportions, the great house, unlike its Federal successors, rarely rose above two stories in height. An excellent example of the great house, contemporary with the Lady Pepperrell House, is the Wentworth-Gardner House (1760) in Portsmouth. Successors of the great house may be seen in such a house as the Peirce Mansion (1799) in Portsmouth, and such a country house as Gore Place (1804) in Waltham, Massachusetts.

THE GREAT HOUSE: THE LADY PEPPERRELL HOUSE, 1760

In 1947, for the first time since the tragic fire of December 27, 1945,[10] the Lady Pepperrell House was open to the public. Once more people strolled through the beautiful garden, entered the inviting gate with its urn topped gateposts flanked by massive shrubbery, proceeded along the beach stone path to the great front door with its heavy knocker which Sarah Orne Jewett tells us frightened her when as a girl she went there to call. To those of us who saw the house after the main hall had been gutted by fire, the beautiful newel post standing intact amidst the ruins, the panelled rooms heavily coated by smoke stain, priceless furnishings battered and charred, it seemed this summer that a miracle had taken place. The old house has been carefully restored by the architect, Frank Chouteau Brown of Boston, and the chief constructor, John Fellows of Kittery *(see Figs. 3 and 4)*. Little evidence remains of the devastation wrought there. The old house appears as lovely as ever. On the afternoon of the fire, the corresponding secretary of the Society for the Preservation of New England Antiquities, William Sumner Appleton of Boston, visited the house. He announced a reconstruction program immediately.

Most of the traditions of the Lady Pepperrell House cluster about two women, Lady Mary Pepperrell and Miss Mary Chauncey Cutts. Lady Mary Pepperrell built this house the year after her husband died; she was fifty-seven years old. She loved her church above all things, which is probably the reason she built her home in this particular location *(see Fig. 2)*. She may have feared lest old age should make it difficult for her to attend services.

Lady Mary Pepperrell was not a native of Kittery. She had been born in Boston where her parents were married by Cotton Mather.[11] Her father, Grove Hirst, a wealthy Boston merchant, born in Salem, married a Boston girl, Elizabeth Sewall. Lady Mary Pepperrell grew up amidst her mother's Boston relatives, her uncle Samuel Sewall, married to Governor Dudley's daughter, her uncle Joseph Sewall, pastor of the Old South Church in Boston, her aunt Gerrish's husband, town clerk of Boston, her uncle Cooper, another Boston pastor. Nor were the family traditions of Lady Mary Pepperrell all immediate. Grandfather Sewall was the same Samuel Sewall whom we recall as the colonial diarist, the judge who was such a "big-minded" man that he publicly confessed in Church his error in the Salem witchcraft trials. Great-grandfather John Hull was

---

[10] See the *Portsmouth Herald*, Dec. 27 – Dec. 28, 1945.
[11] See the footnotes referring to Lady Pepperrell in the Massachusetts Historical Society edition of Sewall's diary.

treasurer of the town of Boston and of the colony of Massachusetts. He was mintmaster, the subject of a delightful story by Hawthorne in the *Tales of a Grandfather's Chair.* Hosts of Sewall cousins helped to swell the family's fame in Boston.

In the midst of this bustling provincial society, Mary Hirst spent her childhood. When she was thirteen, her mother died; when she was fourteen, she lost her father as well. The Hirst children, Samuel and his four sisters Mary, Elizabeth, Hannah and Jane, came to live with their grandfather, the Chief Justice of Massachusetts Bay. Samuel Hirst caused his grandfather grave concern, because of his independence of spirit. At fourteen he entered Harvard where he took his bachelor's and his master's degrees. When he was only twenty-one, with no warning of ill health, he fell dead one day while walking on Long Wharf in Boston. Despite any misgivings they may have had of Samuel, the family was plunged into grief over this tragedy.[12]

Mary Hirst's three sisters married and lived in Boston. Hannah Hirst married a wealthy Boston merchant (Nathaniel Balston) and lived on Beacon Hill. Elizabeth Hirst married the Rev. Charles Chauncey, D.D., a Harvard graduate, pastor of the First Church in Boston. Charles Chauncey was a distinguished parson, the most influential clergyman of his time in Boston, and, with the exception of Jonathan Edwards, in all New England. Chauncey was the acknowledged leader of the liberals of his generation. Jane Hirst married the Rev. Addington Davenport, Jr., a Harvard alumnus, rector of Trinity Church in Boston.[13]

We have a record of the Hirst-Pepperrell marriage from the hand of Lady Pepperrell's kinsman, Samuel Sewall, Jr. He wrote in his diary:

Feb. 21, 1722/3. At night betwixt seven and eight, was married per father Sewall, couz. Mary Hirst to Capt. William Pepperrell of Kittery. Brothers Sewall and Cooper prayed, one before and one after the wedding. Wife and I present, with little Henry. Gave us gloves.[14]

For thirty-seven years Mary Hirst and her husband lived happily together. In 1760, the year after he died, she erected a house near the church. Here she lived in considerable seclusion. When war came her

---

12 The tradition (New England Historical and Genealogical Register, v. 36, p. 193) that Hirst was accidentally buried alive has been repudiated by Shipton in Sibley's Harvard Graduates, v. 7, p. 192.
13 The Davenports' son-in-law, Benjamin Faneuil, whose family gave Faneuil Hall, became a refugee during the Revolution. Elizabeth Hirst Chauncey's only son came to Kittery Point to live near his aunt. His two successive wives, Mary Cutts and Joanna Gerrish, were born in Kittery Point. The Chaunceys lived near Chauncey's Creek which took its name from the family. In 1791, two years after Lady Pepperrell died, Chauncey removed to Portsmouth where he had engaged in business for some time.
14 *Diary of Samuel Sewall.* In *Massachusetts Historical Society Collections,* series 5, v. 5, p. xxxvii.

property was confiscated, but she repurchased it. The Revolutionary War must have caused her great sadness for her family was torn apart and many of them sailed for England, never to return. Lady Mary Pepperrell was granted a pension by the British government as the widow of a baronet.[15·] For some time she paid the largest tax of any person in Kittery.[16] When Washington visited Parson Stevens at Kittery Point in 1789 he walked directly past Lady Pepperrell's house. Washington did not stop, though she was the most prominent person in Kittery. Perhaps the old lady was too ill to see him; perhaps, on the other hand, she was too much of a loyalist. To the close of her days, she may have acknowledged no ruler save King George III.

Lady Pepperrell apparently lived very simply in the days after the Revolutionary War. No doubt a great deal of her income was taken up in assistance to her many relatives impoverished by the American Revolution. She kept but three slaves, Cicero, Zilpah, and Dick, and granted freedom to them before she died, as well as remembering them (including Dick's children) in her will.[17] Others who worked in her house were remembered by her, in the will, while ten pounds sterling went to the Reverend Benjamin Stevens. The generous public philanthropies that characterize the will of Col. William Pepperrell and Sir William Pepperrell are not found in Lady Pepperrell's will. By this time the family estate had shrunk considerably. A small benefaction was left by Lady Pepperrell for the poor of the parish. The house, the chaise, the chariot, harness and horses were all left by Lady Pepperrell to her daughter, Mrs. Nathaniel Sparhawk, a widow when her mother died in 1789.

Elizabeth Pepperrell Sparhawk retained the Lady Pepperrell House for only two years. Mrs. Sparhawk's granddaughter Catherine had married a successful Portsmouth lawyer, Daniel Humphreys.[18] Mrs. Sparhawk, in 1791, sold the Lady Pepperrell House to Humphreys who handled the legal and financial business of the Pepperrells through most of his life. Six years later Mrs. Sparhawk died in Boston. For nine years, the Humphreys lived at the Lady Pepperrell House. They had extensive property holdings in Conway, ·New Hampshire, with several other members of the Sparhawk family. Eventually most of the Sparhawks who had Conway holdings went there to live.[19]

---

[15] See Jones, *The Loyalists of Massachusetts*, p. 232.
[16] See Kittery tax lists, published in the issues of *Old Eliot*.
[17] *York County Wills*, v. 38, pp. 78-79.
[18] Daniel Humphreys (Derby, Conn., 1770 - Portsmouth, N. H., 1800), Yale alumnus, studied law in New Haven and kept a private school in New York. Humphreys opened a law office in Portsmouth and was appointed by President Washington U. S. District Attorney for the District of New Hampshire.
[19] See Howard, *Materials for a Genealogy of the Sparhawk Family.*

When Daniel Humphreys left Kittery, he sold the Lady Pepperrell House to another member of the Pepperrell family, Joseph Cutts of Cutts Island, a wealthy and enterprising thirty-six year old merchant who brought his wife and two children here.[20] Joseph Cutts was a great-nephew of Sir William Pepperrell and his wife, Mary Chauncey Cutts, a great-niece of Lady Pepperrell, so it seemed appropriate that the Cutts should occupy the Lady Pepperrell House.[21]

Joseph Cutts' wharf and warehouses stood near the Lady Pepperrell House. His ships engaged in trade with Europe and the West Indies. For a short time, while the Cutts family were at the height of their affluence, the house was the center of magnificent hospitality and rich living. Joseph Cutts' tombstone tells the tragic story of the ending of this fortune:

Captain Cutts was of honorable descent from the early settlers of this region and highly esteemed as a worthy, patriotic and public-spirited citizen, a generous friend and patron of enlightened and general education, sound morals and religion. By his superior energy and judgment and skill as a Merchant, he amassed much wealth but which he irrevocably lost, chiefly through the Embargo Act of 1807 and by the war with Great Britain in 1812.[22]

Jefferson's embargo of 1807 crippled most of the New England shipping. Some daring privateersmen made fortunes out of the War of 1812, but merchants who were unwilling to engage in privateering or whose ships were not fitted for that work were ruined. Captain Cutts, as a measure of precaution, took his vessels up Chauncey's Creek and anchored them behind Gerrish Island.[23] It was necessary to remove the Gerrish Island bridge to get them past. There they rode at anchor and rotted while Joseph Cutts' investments collapsed. In one lawsuit alone the brig *Olive Branch,* the brig *Sally,* the schooner *Dover,* the wharf, the store and its contents, and the dwelling house and lands of Joseph Cutts were seized for debt. Thomas G. Thornton, Marshal of Maine, was the receiver.[24] From 1813 to 1825, the estate was in the hands of the government though the family continued to live there. In 1825, Miss Sarah Chauncey Cutts, Captain Cutts' daughter, purchased the house, store and wharf of the Marshal of Maine.

20 Two other children were born in this house to the Cutts family.
21 Joseph was grandson of Mary Pepperrell Frost; Mary was granddaughter of Elizabeth Hirst Chauncey.
22 Epitaph on Cutts tombstone, burial ground of the First Parish Church, Kittery Point. For further data on Captain Cutts, see references to him in Howard, *The Cutts Family in America.*
23 Reminiscences of Martin Luther Frisbee, in *The Island and Harbor Echo,* v. 4, no. 1, p. 8.
24 Cutts MSS, Joseph W. Cutts, Braemere, Kittery Point.

In 1812, at the height of Captain Cutts' financial difficulties, Mrs. Cutts died. Apparently, the relatives were devoted to each other. When financial misfortunes were crowned by the mother's death, insanity overtook them all.[25] Captain Cutts became mentally deranged; he lived at the house, which was then known as the Cutts Mansion, till his death in 1861, unable to do anything, a care to his daughter Miss Sally who longest of all the family retained her mind.

With little or no financial support, it must have been difficult for Miss Sally to care for her father and her brother Charles. Charles, too, was insane; of the four in his family who lost their reason, only Charles became violent. Charles lived to be sixty-four years old, chained to the floor in one of the upstairs chambers of the mansion house for many, many years, with only Miss Sally to care for him.

In 1839, Miss Sally's brother Joseph, a lieutenant in the Navy stationed at the Navy Yard at Portsmouth, N. H., came home to visit his family. Miss Sally was walking about downstairs when she heard Joseph call her. She went to the foot of the great staircase, and his voice came down: "Do you need me, Sally?" Thinking that he was under the delusion that she had called, Miss Sally replied "No, Joseph." At once he said again: "Do you need me, Sally?" Thinking that he had not heard her answer, she replied again "No, Joseph." She had been busy but a few minutes more when once again she heard the voice: "Do you need me, Sally?" Somewhat puzzled, she replied for the third time, "No, Joseph." Hardly had she answered when a shot rang out from the room above. Miss Sally rushed upstairs to find that her brother had taken his life.

When Joseph died, Miss Sally's world closed in. For her the clock stopped. She remained a great lady, genteel in her bearing, kindly in her manner, but the present no longer existed for her. As the years passed by, her talk was of persons who had died long, long ago as though they were still living.

Samuel Adams Drake has recorded his impressions of Miss Sally Cutts:

Poor Sally Cutts! She rose to take leave of us with the same ceremonious politeness which had marked my reception. Her slight and shrunken figure was long in my memory, her crazy buffet, and broken, antiquated chairs, to which she clung as the most precious of earthly possessions. It was one of her hallucinations to be always expecting the arrival of a messenger from Washington with full reparation of the broken fortunes of her family. Some charitable souls cared for her necessities, but such was the poor creature's pride that artifice was necessary to effect their purpose.[26]

25 Reminiscences of the late Miss Caroline Lewis Gerrish.
26 Drake, *Nooks and Corners of the New England Coast,* p. 144.

In 1866, Miss Sally was pronounced by the Court "non compos mentis" and a guardian appointed so that her support might be assured. The house was sold, with the reservation that Miss Sally might occupy it at an annual rent of $30 per year "so long as in the judgment of her friends and the selectmen of said Kittery it may be deemed for her interest and comfort to so occupy the same."[27] Finally it was found necessary to take Miss Sally to some other house to live. She was unhappy from the time she arrived and longed to be home again. One day she ran away; when she was finally found, Miss Sally was seated in one of the broad window seats of the Lady Pepperrell House nodding genially to all of the passers-by. The house had been locked and barred but Miss Sally had entered a window, opened up the shutters and again become the mistress of the great house.

After Miss Sally died, in 1874, the house remained unoccupied for four years. Caleb Eastman of York, Miss Sally's guardian, secured the property from William Wentworth Cutts of Kittery who purchased it during Miss Sally's lifetime. The house changed hands several times but always among members of the Cutts family.[28]

Since the time when Joseph Cutts lost his fortune in 1812, the old house had received no care; it was fast advancing into a state of dilapidation. In 1888, J. Chester Cutts purchased the place and commenced to restore it.[29] Mr. Cutts, with his large family of children (most of whom are still living) brought life and activity to the Lady Pepperrell House. They loved the old house which was to them an ancestral home. It was furnished with appropriate pieces brought from their Cutts Island house which had been torn down.

In 1922, Mr. Cutts sold the Lady Pepperrell House to William Wilson Wood, 3rd,[30] of "Arrowston," Piqua, Ohio. Mr. Wood remembered this vicinity for as a boy he had studied at Phillips Exeter Academy nearby. In 1922, he retired from the presidency of the Wood Shovel and Tool Company of Piqua and became chairman of the board of this firm. At the same time, he moved to Kittery Point. With a fortune at his command, Mr. Wood made the Lady Pepperrell House a "show-place." He laid out the present garden above the top of which he could see from the upstairs windows his steam yacht riding at anchor in the harbor. He added porches flanking the house and acquired a number of original furnishings.

27 *York Deeds*, v. 296, p. 268.
28 Members of the Cutts family who owned the house included George S. Cutts of Exeter, Oliver Cutts of Kittery (who owned Deering Tavern), and J. Chester Cutts of Kittery.
29 Information furnished by Joseph W. Cutts.
30 See William Wilson Wood III, in *Who's Who in American Commerce and Industry*, v. 4 (1944), p. 1101.

After eight years, involving considerable expenditure, Mr. Wood sold the house to Virginia L. Hodge (Mrs. Lovell Hodge) of Philadelphia, a descendant of Washington's sister.[31] Mrs. Hodge brought to the Lady Pepperrell House the traditions of Virginia hospitality and fine living, ably assisted by her friend Miss Katherine Parry, a descendant of the Waldrons of New Hampshire. Mrs. Hodge, in December 1942, presented the Lady Pepperrell House to the Society for the Preservation of New England Antiquities. It was furnished for the society by Mrs. Hodge and Miss Parry.

---

[31] Mrs. Hodge's ancestress, Betty Washington, married Col. Fielding Lewis of "Kenmore"; some of the furnishings of the Lady Pepperrell House are Washington and Lewis pieces.

THE EARLY MANSION

The distinguishing features of a mansion in colonial times appear to have been the quality of woodwork and furnishings. Certainly many country houses of ample proportions, equal in size to the mansions, were referred to as farm houses, while houses no larger than these, with highly decorative woodwork, panelling, wainscotting, cornices, mantels, balusters, and brasses, became mansions.

Some of the mansions, like Pepperrell Mansion, despite the early date of building, possessed magnificent interiors with woodwork that has never been excelled. Often these mansions were surrounded by many acres of land, while a large number of employees depended on the estate for a livelihood.

THE EARLY MANSION: PEPPERRELL MANSION, 1682

Pepperrell Mansion, in Kittery Point, at the height of its prosperity, between 1725 and 1775, was one of the great houses of colonial America *(see Figs. 5 and 6)*. The Pepperrells had amassed a princely fortune and won considerable fame. They were landholders with an estate that stretched for thirty miles along the Maine coast.[32] Their vessels sailed from Portsmouth Harbor to the Indies and to Europe. Their home at Kittery Point was based on the English way of life—fully panelled walls and many portraits, liveried servants, the master's barge, his deer park and his gardens.[33]

The builder of this house, Col. William Pepperrell of Revelstoke, Devon, first settled at Appledore Island, in the Isles of Shoals just off Kittery Point. Kittery Point was a veritable bit of Devon transplanted. Robert Cutts from Estonwell, Francis Champernowne from Dartington, Alexander Shapleigh[34] from Kingsweare, Roger Deering from Dartmouth, and John Bray from Plymouth, were the largest landholders on this heavily wooded and but half-cleared shore, named after a manor on the river Dart in Devon. When Pepperrell married beautiful Margery Bray of Kittery Point, his father-in-law deeded to him the land for a home next to his own. Here, in 1682, Pepperrell Mansion was built, looking out over Tavistock Island and the meeting of the Piscataqua River with the sea.

Col. Pepperrell lived to see his ships sail to England and beyond, and when he died, he remembered the poor of Revelstoke in his will.[35] Toward the close of a busy life in which he had built up one of the great colonial shipping firms—after he had served as colonel in command of the Kittery militia and as judge of the Court of Common Pleas— Pepperrell considered retiring and returning to his Devon home. Though he took steps to purchase property in Devon,[36] he died here and left his estate to his son who was born in this house and was always an American colonial.

Sir William Pepperrell, first American to be created a British baronet, first American to be created a general in the British royal army, won these awards by the capture of the French fortress of Louisbourg.

32 Nettels, *The Roots of American Civilization*, pp. 626-7.
33 Stevens, *The First American Baronet*. In *The Magazine of American History*, v. 2 (1878), pp. 683-4.
34 Shapleigh at one time owned most of Kittery Point. He was one of the few emigrants to America to arrive in his own ship.
35 See the references to the will of Col. William Pepperrell in Parsons, *Life of Sir William Pepperrell, Bart.*
36 References to Pepperrell's intention of returning to England are found in Parsons, *Life of Sir William Pepperrell, Bart.*

The victorious siege gave the colonials a feeling of confidence which they never forgot and of which they made good use later. Louisbourg had cost Louis XIV the equivalent of ten million dollars to build. So expensive it seemed to the Sun King, he is said to have quipped that he hoped from the shores of France to see it rising up out of the sea.

Sir William Pepperrell was for many years president of the governor's council, and, for a few months, acting governor of Massachusetts. Lady Pepperrell, born Mary Hirst of Boston, was granddaughter of diarist Judge Samuel Sewall and Mintmaster John Hull. At their Kittery Point home, the Pepperrells were hosts to noted contemporaries including Sir Peter Warren, Cotton Mather, George Whitefield the evangelist, Governors Walcott, Shirley, and John and Benning Wentworth.

The second Sir William Pepperrell was born William Pepperrell Sparhawk, but changed his name when he inherited the Pepperrell fortune from his grandfather. After being graduated from Harvard, he married a daughter of Gen. Isaac Royall of Antigua and Royall House, Medford, Massachusetts, and brought her to Pepperrell Mansion, where their children were born and where they were to know but a few years of happiness. Young Pepperrell served as royal councillor and for his services was created a baronet, in 1774, on the eve of the American Revolution.[37] The Pepperrells, being loyalists, left their Kittery Point home for Boston and shortly thereafter for England. Lady Pepperrell died on the way and was buried at St. Paul's Church, Halifax. The second Sir William Pepperrell[38] led the loyalist cause in England but it was a lost cause. He was an English army officer and one of the founders of the British Foreign Bible Society. He did not return to America; only one of his descendants lives on this side of the Atlantic today, the present Lord Bishop of Newfoundland.[39]

Shortly after the Pepperrells left for England their property was confiscated by the Massachusetts Confiscation Act. Pepperrell Mansion became a barracks for Revolutionary troops who were organized here and marched from here to battle for the patriot cause. The house was occupied by Joshua Fernald[40] one of the patriots who returned from the war. Joshua Fernald had seen service with the Massachusetts

37 The *Annual Register for the Year 1774*, p. 188.
38 For biographical details on the second Sir William Pepperrell, see Sabine, *The American Loyalists*, and Jones, *The Loyalists of Massachusetts*.
39 The Rt. Rev. Philip Selwyn Abraham, Lord Bishop of Newfoundland.
40 See Fernald, *Life of Elder Mark Fernald*, and Safford, *Historic Homes of Kittery*. For biographical information on Fernald, Smallcorn, and Cutts, see Remick, *A Record of the Services of the Commissioned Officers and Enlisted Men of Kittery and Eliot, Who Served Their Country on Land and Sea in the American Revolution from 1775 to 1783*.

State Troops in Connecticut and New York, and then sailed under
Capt. Thomas Thompson of Portsmouth in the Kittery-built frigate
Raleigh when she fought H.M.S. *Druid* on the high seas. Joshua's
son Elder Mark Fernald tells, in his autobiography, of his birth in
Pepperrell Mansion. Elder Fernald, a noted preacher in his day, was
one of the founders of the Christian Church in Maine. First purchaser
of the mansion, Capt. Samuel Smallcorn, formerly an officer on the
Raleigh, had engaged in privateering. Smallcorn in October, 1793,
bought the house of the Commonwealth of Massachusetts which had
confiscated it. The following month Capt. Smallcorn sold the house
to Maj. Thomas Donnell Cutts, who (like his father Capt. Thomas
Cutts of Kittery) had served in the Revolutionary War. Major Cutts
remodeled the old store (still standing) at the entrance to Frisbee's
Wharf, and kept there a store, while he had a tavern at the mansion.
The major set out many elm trees on the property, a few of which
are still standing. After financial difficulties, Thomas Donnell Cutts
mortgaged the place, and the mortgage was foreclosed. Pepperrell
Mansion passed to a distant relative of T. D. Cutts, Richard Cutts
of Cutts Island, brother of the owner of the Lady Pepperrell House.
Richard Cutts' mother was a great-niece of Sir William Pepperrell,
so, for a few years the house returned to the Pepperrell family. Richard Cutts was a merchant engaged in foreign trade. Since he already
owned the Cutts Island property, he disposed of Pepperrell Mansion
to Elder Jesse Meader and Capt. Jesse Frisbee.

After Capt. Frisbee was lost at sea, Elder Meader and the Frisbee
heirs sold Pepperrell Mansion to the Hon. Charles C. Bellamy[41] and
Thomas 0. Hoyt.[42] In 1848, the new owners removed 15 feet from the
east end of the house and 10 feet from the west end, leaving it nearly
the same size as it was before the first Sir William made additions to
it.[43] Thomas Hoyt sold his share of the house to Bellamy, in 1845.

Senator Bellamy (or Squire Bellamy, as he was familiarly called
in shortening the English Esquire) entertained here many political
figures of his time, Governor Fairfield of Maine, James C. Blaine,
Hannibal Hamlin, Judge Nathan Clifford, and William Pitt Fessen-
den. Pepperrell Mansion was the home, throughout the greater part

41 Hon. Charles G. Bellamy (Kittery Point, 1811 - Kittery Point, 1899) was son of John and Tamsen
(Haley) Bellamy of Kittery. Further biographical data on Bellamy will be found elsewhere in this book.
42 See footnote 5.
43 The portions removed from the Pepperrell Mansion were used in two houses erected at about 1848.
One house was owned by the Frisbee family and has been destroyed by fire. The second house, erected
by Thomas O. Hoyt, is now the home of his granddaughter Cora Hoyt Blake (Mrs. Melvin Blake).
44 See biographical articles on Bellamy, in *Antiques Magazine,* listed in the bibliography.

of his life, of Senator Bellamy's son, the woodcarver, John Haley Bellamy, whose figureheads have graced the seven seas.[44] John Haley Bellamy was the greatest carver of ship's figureheads America has produced. Eagles carved by Bellamy are today collectors' items. Bellamy did his carving in the little building made from Sir William Pepperrell's counting house which stands at the water's edge, before Pepperrell Mansion *(see Fig. 7)*. This little building in summer was the frequent rendezvous of an interesting group of friends, Bellamy, Mark Twain, George Wasson, William Dean Howells, and Winslow Homer. After John Haley Bellamy died, in 1914, his family continued to live in the Pepperrell Mansion which became the property of his niece and nephews, Mrs. Alonzo Wildes of Kittery, Maine, Dr. Victor Safford of Jamaica Plain, Mass., and the late Eugene Williams of Kittery, who lived in the house until his death.

In 1945, when Pepperrell Mansion was purchased from the Bellamy heirs by Martin Frost of Frost Garrisons, Eliot, it returned again to the family of the builder, Col. William Pepperrell of Revelstoke, Devon. The property has been completely restored, since 1945, and is now occupied by Mr. Frost, Mrs. Lovell Hodge, and Miss Katherine Parry.

Many features combine to make Pepperrell Mansion an architectural gem, heavy cornices and fragile balusters, a well-proportioned hallway with a spacious landing, an entrance doorway topped with bull's-eye panes of glass, a beehive closet with scalloped shelves, and everywhere panelling in lavish profusion. Though Pepperrell Mansion is not a large house, a single glance at its interior tells one much of the accomplishments and taste of its builder.

THE LATE MANSION

It will seem to some persons to be drawing too fine a distinction to mark off an early colonial mansion and a late colonial mansion. Actually, there is little difference between them outside of the historical date attached to them. The late mansion made slightly more of an attempt to achieve the grandiose than did its predecessor. This is evident in Sparhawk Hall where the council chamber, resembling the ballroom of a Southern mansion (for example, the ballroom at Hampton Plantation, South Carolina) fills one end of the house, on the ground floor.

Sparhawk Hall has been fortunate in retaining its grounds; the fields provide a beautiful setting for the old house which is reminiscent of some of the very small country estates to be seen occasionally in England.

THE LATE MANSION: SPARHAWK HALL, 1742

Unlike most colonial houses of Kittery Point, Sparhawk Hall[45] is rarely seen by the traveller who is not searching for it. Just past the parish church on Pepperrell Road, a well concealed drive bursts through the heavy foliage, and the passerby catches a gleam of warm yellow and white at the end of a long driveway. It is the main entrance to Sparhawk Hall *(see Fig. 8)*.

When, in 1742, William Pepperrell built Sparhawk Hall as a wedding gift for his daughter Elizabeth, the house was approached by a long avenue of trees stretching from the hall to Pepperrell Mansion more than a quarter of a mile away. The hall was planned as a model of elegance for its day, even as Pepperrell Mansion expressed the highest reaches achieved in American colonial building in its day. Massive trees were hewn from the Pepperrell forest and shipped to England for finishing.

Throughout the house today, the evidences of late provincial grandeur are unmistakable. In a broad hallway with panelled wainscotting, the stairs, with elaborately carved balusters, sweep gracefully to a broad landing crowned by a Palladian window *(see Fig. 9)*. The interior is so little changed from its original appearance that it is easy to pick out accretions by which later owners have marked their individual interests and tastes. Surmounting the newel post is a pineapple by Bellamy, famed carver of ship's figureheads. A Bellamy hawk perched upon a spar, swings gracefully in the stairwell. These significantly appropriate additions, suggested by the armorial bearings of the Pepperrells and Sparhawks, were introduced by the late Hon. Horace Mitchell.

The exterior of the house is much the same as when it was built. The main house has retained its original dimensions, 60'x 34'. The doorway is topped by bull's-eye panes of glass, and the mansard roof is pierced by luthern windows just as was the mansard roof of Pepperrell Mansion till the alterations of 1848. The cupola that surmounts Sparhawk Hall is in unpleasing disproportion to the rest of the house. It was added by the English Browns replacing an earlier cupola.

The full eastern end of the house is taken up by the council chamber, panelled from floor to ceiling. The council chamber is a pleasant room, but all of the rooms of this house are pleasant. One can sit in the window seats of any room in Sparhawk Hall and look out across former Sparhawk acres.

---

45 Much of the information on Sparhawk Hall was furnished by Miss C. L. Gerrish, Gertrude Chase Mitchell (Mrs. Horace Mitchell), and Martin Frost.

Partly the setting, partly the house itself, both so English, both so Georgian, take one's mind across three thousand miles of sea. To Nathaniel Sparhawk and his bride, to their children as well, England was a generation or two away, at most, and London was the capital and center of civilization. Nathaniel Sparhawk was a dandy. He was fond of coach and show. He loved his way of life as his letters indicate. His efforts as a merchant were crowned with bankruptcy. His style and pride and business dealings were but little appreciated by his contemporaries. When he died, in 1776, he was interred in the Pepperrell tomb and some of his contemporaries scratched upon the tomb a verse playing upon his name:

> Here lies the hawk, who in his day,
> Made many an honest bird his prey;
> But now he's gone and unlamented,
> Heaven be praised — We're all contented.
> Heaven is pleased when sinners cease from sin
> And Hell exalts when villains enter in.

But we must not be too hard on Nathaniel Sparhawk. His ambition was to live as an English gentleman. The fulfillment of his ambition was thwarted by financial reversals. He must have served creditably as a member of the royal governor's council for he was appointed to it eleven times. He was also colonel of a regiment of Massachusetts militia, representative to the general court for many years, and justice of the Court of Common Pleas. He lived to see his family completely separated by the American revolution.

Though the Sparhawks had seven children, but five of them lived to maturity. The second Nathaniel Sparhawk inherited Sparhawk Hall. His brother William Pepperrell Sparhawk became the second Sir William Pepperrell of London. Another brother Andrew changed his name to Pepperrell. Andrew Pepperrell married and lived in Portsmouth, New Hampshire.[46] Andrew[47] was proscribed as a royalist by the New Hampshire court and banished from the province. He attempted to return to his home, in 1778, but was imprisoned in Portsmouth. Only his prestige eventually effected his release. Andrew returned to England where he received a commission in the British

---

[46] The Andrew Pepperrell House in New Castle, N. H., was not the home of young Andrew Pepperrell but of his great-uncle, Capt. Andrew Pepperrell (a brother of Sir William Pepperrell), a wealthy merchant. Andrew's son-in-law, Capt. William Wentworth (a brother of Governor Benning Wentworth) received his estate. It is now the summer home of Mr. and Mrs. George H. Warren of Manchester, N. H. New Castle was also the home of Andrew's sister Mary, wife of Hon. John Frost. Their home at New Castle, Frost Point, was demolished by the owner, Miss Frances Grier, in 1945, as it had deteriorated. It stood at the entrance to the driveway of Miss Anne C. Withington.

[47] For information on Andrew Pepperrell, see references to him in Jones, *The Loyalists of Massachusetts*.

army, and finally died in London.[48] A third brother, Samuel Hirst
Sparhawk, a Harvard alumnus, became a royalist and fled to England
but later returned to Kittery Point, where he died in 1789. He was the
father of Harriet Hirst Sparhawk, a natural daughter born in England,
by whom it is not known; this daughter was left a substantial estate
by her father. Harriet Hirst Sparhawk [49] died at her home, 2 Sheafe
Street, in Portsmouth, in 1871, leaving a small amount of property to
her cousins. She repaired the Pepperrell tomb and was the last of Sir
William Pepperrell's descendants to be interred in the tomb.

The youngest of the children of Col. Nathaniel and Elizabeth
Sparhawk was the beautiful daughter Miss Mary Pepperrell Sparhawk. Tradition tells us that she saved Portsmouth from destruction
by the British.[50] Capt. Mowatt of the *Canceaux*, a British eighteen-gun
war ship, sailed into Portsmouth Harbor plotting the destruction of
the town. He stopped at the pro-royalist Sparhawk home in Kittery
Point and was so charmed by the personality of Miss Mary Pepperrell
Sparhawk that he sailed to Falmouth and burned that town instead.
Mary later married one of the most ardent and most noted of Boston
patriots, Dr. Charles Jarvis, a physician, surgeon, and statesman, who
was a delegate to the Constitutional Convention. As a widow, she
returned to Sparhawk Hall, where she died childless in 1815.

After Col. Nathaniel Sparhawk died, Sparhawk Hall became the
home of the second Nathaniel Sparhawk and his three successive wives.
Nathaniel Sparhawk Jr. was a royalist in sympathies but, for some unknown reason, was not banished. Sparhawk Hall should have been a
happy place with six children to play about the mansion house, but the
ominous approach of war and domestic difficulties prevented happiness.
Nathaniel and Catherine, his first wife, made the place a Tory center.
Tradition tells us that it was an underground station for Tories escaping
the fury of the patriots. Be that as it may, Nathaniel Sparhawk's business
was ruined by the war and by the hatred his sympathies won for him. He
pleaded in England for compensation for losses sustained while uphold-
ing the king's cause. He says that he was much mistreated by his neigh-

[48] Andrew Pepperrell's wife Anne (Mary Ann Turner), was the daughter of Capt. George Turner, a
British officer stationed in Portsmouth. Anne was a loyalist and died in Chelsea, London, childless.
Anne's sister Margaret was the wife of a prominent Portsmouth, N. H. patriot, Capt. Thomas Thompson,
a native of Dartmouth, England. Thompson was captain of the *Raleigh* and a Portsmouth shipbuilder
and merchant. As Grand Master of Masons in New Hampshire, in 1807, Thompson laid the corner-stone
of St. John's Church, Portsmouth.
[49] Administration was granted, Oct. 3, 1871, on the estate of Harriet Hirst Sparhawk (Rockingham
County Probate Records, Exeter, N. H., Estate No. 514½). An obituary notice of Miss Harriet appeared in
the *New England Historical and Genealogical Register*, v. 25, no. 4 (Oct. 1871), p. 400.
[50] For a full discussion of this tradition, see the *New England Historical and Genealogical Register*, v. 27,
no. 3 (July 1873), pp. 256-266.

bors. For a while Nathaniel fled to Salem and lived there. A third marriage being unhappy, Nathaniel went to England to be near his brothers, taking his daughter Susan with him. Young Susan died of smallpox in London, and Nathaniel returned to die at Kittery Point in the same year, in the same house as his sister Mrs. Jarvis. The Sparhawks had been stripped of their fortunes almost overnight. Save for the fortunate marriages of Nathaniel's three daughters, his grandchildren would have been penniless. Nathaniel Sparhawk Jr. was the last of the Sparhawks to live at Sparhawk Hall. The valuation of his estate, in 1815, reached but $2234.97, and claims of $1961.67 were advanced against it.[51] Among the claims is listed the cost of his funeral; the charges amounted to but $24. The widow was now free to wed, and she married and went to live in Andover, Massachusetts. Perhaps she had never been happy as the mistress of Sparhawk Hall in its decline.

Sparhawk Hall was sold at public auction for but a thousand dollars to a Portsmouth merchant and shipowner, Hon. James Sheafe[52] former U.S. Senator from New Hampshire. Senator Sheafe had built a large brick town house in Portsmouth and had extensive property besides. His wife (the former Sarah Meserve) was no stranger to Kittery Point where her grandfather Rev. John Newmarch was the first clergyman. The Sheafes had been loyalists. Like many another loyalist, Sheafe was not obvious about his sympathies. He was allowed to remain unmolested though his father-in-law when appointed stamp collector was burned in effigy by a Portsmouth mob. Sheafe himself was summoned before the Committee of Safety at Exeter.

The Sheafes had owned Sparhawk Hall for less than a month when they were offered $1400 for it. They accepted the offer made by Joshua T. Chase of Kittery who occupied the house for nine years.[53] For a while, ownership of the house, revolved among Chase, Robert Gerrish Safford, and Roger Dearing.[54] In 1845, Dearing was in full possession. Roger Dearing was a veteran of the War of 1812; he had fought in the engagement between the *Enterprise* and the *Boxer*.[55] He brought to Sparhawk Hall a large family of children of whom three became physicians of note.

[51] York County Probate Records, Alfred, Maine, v. 25, pp. 371-2.
[52] For information on Sheafe, see references to him in Brewster, *Rambles about Portsmouth*.
[53] Joshua Chase was a grandson of the first Congregational clergyman in Kittery Foreside, and a son-in-law of this man's successor.
[54] In 1836, the Chases sold the house to Safford and Dearing, and, in 1838, Dearing sold his part to Safford; in 1841, again the Chases sold the house to Safford and Dearing, and, in 1845, Safford sold his half to Dearing. Safford moved to Wisconsin. Safford and Dearing had married sisters from York, Maine, by the name of Boston.
[55] Stackpole, *Old Kittery and Her Families*, p. 343.

In 1851, for $1800, Sparhawk Hall was sold to Elizabeth Stark Newell of Boston. Mrs. Newell was own granddaughter of Gen. John Stark of Bennington fame whose words have been repeated many times: "Tonight we beat the British, boys, or Molly Stark's a widow."[56] Handsome Mrs. Newell was wed to an East India merchant of Boston who was also postmaster of Cambridge. Sparhawk Hall had been theirs but two years when a tragedy occurred. At Andover, Mass., a railroad accident took place. Mr. Newell was brought from the wreckage living, but he survived for only a short while. Within five months of his death, Mrs. Newell sold Sparhawk Hall.[57]

The Penhallows, who purchased Sparhawk Hall from Mrs. Newell, were Portsmouth people of considerable prominence. Capt. Pearce Wentworth Penhallow of Portsmouth, Boston, and Liverpool, England, was a sea captain who commanded his own ship at the age of twenty-three. His wife, Elizabeth Warner Pitts Sherburne Penhallow, was a descendant of Mary Pepperrell Frost, Sir William Pepperrell's sister. The Penhallows lived at Sparhawk Hall for twelve years.

When the Penhallows disposed of Sparhawk Hall, in 1869, it was purchased for $3000 by a Toronto banker, Walter Richard Brown, who shortly afterwards turned it over to his English born wife, Jane Selina Akrill Brown. Since the Browns maintained considerable seclusion, not a great deal is known of them. They filled Sparhawk Hall with beautiful furnishings, including many fine paintings and engravings. Having no children, they adopted a daughter Emily, who died five years after they moved to Kittery Point, when she was but eleven years old. Mr. Brown's death was followed by Mrs. Brown's insanity. At the request of friends and neighbors, Harrison Jesse Philbrick of Kittery was appointed Mrs. Brown's guardian. For the last nine years of Mrs. Brown's life, Sparhawk Hall was closed much of the time; she lived at Mr. Philbrick's home, Whipple Garrison, in Kittery. When Mrs. Brown died, in 1899, difficulty was experienced in locating heirs. A sister, Anne Eliza Newcomen of Warwick and Birmingham, England, was still living but was "non compos mentis." Three nephews were living, Joseph Akrill of Lincoln, England (natural son of Mrs. Brown's sister), Joseph Lomas Akrill of Brooklyn, N. Y., and John Akrill, "address unknown." John Akrill was never located. Until sufficient time had elapsed, the Mitchells (next owners of Sparhawk Hall) were unable to have a clear title to their property.

---

[56] Stark's observation is sometimes recorded as: "There, my boys, are your enemies, the red-coats and tories. You must beat them or my wife sleeps a widow tonight."
[57] See Emery, *Newell Ancestry*, for further data on the Newell family.

In 1902, Hon. Horace Mitchell of Kittery purchased Sparhawk Hall. Mr. Mitchell, who for some years was state senator from Kittery, was a well-known hotel proprietor in New England, till his death in 1922. Having for five years managed the Hotel Pocahontas at Gerrish Island, in 1890 he erected the Champernowne at Kittery Point across the highway from Sparhawk Hall. A well-known figure in the East, Mr. Mitchell was host at Sparhawk Hall to President William Howard Taft and Secretary of State Philander Knox upon their state visit to Kittery.

The present owner of Sparhawk Hall, Horace Mitchell Jr., is a descendant of Andrew Pepperrell.[58] Mr. Mitchell is editor and proprietor of the Kittery Press, an editor of Sports Afield, and a writer on game breeding and preservation. Both Mr. and Mrs. Mitchell are interested in this historic house, and, in 1947, have renovated the building.

[58] Mr. Mitchell, through his mother, the late Gertrude Chase Mitchell, is a descendant of Andrew Pepperrell.

THE GARRISON

Garrison houses are, generally speaking, of three types: (1) a building designed for fighting purposes with thick timbered walls pierced by portholes, (2) a building designed to serve both as a residence in time of peace and a refuge in time of war (often constructed with overhang), and (3) a building centrally located and designated by the town as one of the places of refuge in the event of an Indian attack. Frost Garrisons, in Eliot, Maine, erected in 1734-38, illustrates the first type of garrison. The Mcintire Garrison, in York, Maine, erected 1657, illustrates the second type of garrison. Mitchell Garrison, erected around 1700, illustrates the third type of garrison. I know of only one garrison with portholes preserved as a museum, but it is a worthy example, the Dam-Drew Garrison (1675) now a part of the Woodman Institute in Dover, N.H.

Unfortunately, the garrison had neither shingles nor clapboards to protect it from the weather; often the sills rested on the ground so that in damp weather the sills rotted. As a result we have few of the large number of colonial garrisons left. The necessity for garrisons in New England passed before the American Revolution arrived. It may be helpful in connection with garrisons to review the major Indian Wars:

(1) King William's War (in Europe the War of the League of Augsburg, 1689-97)

(2) Queen Anne's War (in Europe the War of the Spanish Succession, 1702-13)

(3) King George's War (in Europe the War of the Austrian Succession, 1744-48)

(4) French and Indian War (in Europe the Seven Years' War, 1756-1763)

THE GARRISON: MITCHELL GARRISON, c. 1700

One of the most interesting buildings in Maine has an illusive history. If we trace its history before 1768, we are making a guess. If we say that a fort sat on the site before the garrison was erected, we are again hazarding a guess. We are not, however, guessing without reason for we have much evidence that would lead to the probability that here is the Joseph Mitchell garrison *(see Fig. 10)*, built on the site of an earlier fort, possibly the work of his grandfather Christopher Mitchell.

For a long while little was known of Mitchell Garrison. The driveway appears to the passing motorist to be the driveway to another house. Even after proceeding a short distance up the drive, it appears to be a rough woods road. The car must go almost a quarter of a mile through woods till a clearing appears. On the crest of a rise sits the Mitchell Garrison. For many years this place was known only to natives who referred to it as "Tommy Grant's Beeches" because of the beautiful grove of beech trees that stretches from here to Bartlett Road.

Around 1937, Mitchell Garrison was visited by two persons interested in preserving historic buildings, Luke Vincent Lockwood of New York and Miss Elizabeth Perkins of New York and York Village, Maine. After examining the two rooms with handhewn log walls, located above ground level, they passed below into the cellar. Here, much to their surprise, they found that the cellar walls resembled more nearly the earthworks of a fort than ordinary cellar construction, and indicated that the building or its site had once been used as a fort. This theory was given further evidence when an examination of the elevation on which the building was erected indicated that the knoll was, in part, of artificial construction. Miss Perkins was much interested in acquiring title to the property to form a part of the group of buildings owned by Historic Landmarks, Inc. Before she was able to take steps to purchase the property, it had passed from the receiver's hands into the possession of Col. Winthrop Lee Biddle of Cynwyd, Pennsylvania.

Col. Biddle and his family spent some time at Kittery and hoped to make Kittery their home, for they were fond of the old garrison. When business interests took Col. Biddle to Chicago, the house again fell vacant. Once more it passed into receivership and was advertised for sale at public auction. Shortly before the auction in the summer of 1947, Elizabeth R. Buswell (Mrs. Richmond Buswell) who had spent several years in Portsmouth, visited the property. She was searching for a house of historic interest in this vicinity which she could restore as a home. Mrs. Buswell was delighted with Mitchell Garrison and made an offer which was accepted by Miss Rosamond Thaxter who handled the real estate transaction.

Mitchell Garrison is a one-story building (two rooms without a hallway) and a garret reached by a ladder. One wall of panelling within the building was placed there in recent years by Col. Biddle. A massive center chimney pierces the building. The house is extremely simple, erected in proportions similar to those of the Dam-Drew Garrison (now in Woodman Institute) of Dover. It is in Kittery but close to the York boundary in the district known as Seabury. Not far away, but across the town boundary, is the historic Raynes house. Both are located near Braveboat Harbor.

Christopher Mitchell appears in Kittery records in 1660. His home was at the head of Braveboat Harbor where he lived with his wife and ten children. Among the children of Christopher Mitchell was a son Joseph who was carried captive to Canada by the Indians, and was held captive in Canada in October, 1695.[59] He must have soon after returned and married Joanna Couch, for the eldest of his nine children was born in 1703. Joseph Mitchell's captivity occurred shortly after the Candlemas Day massacre at York nearby, in 1692, when according to Francis Hooke of Kittery, 137 persons were either killed or taken captive.

When a list of Kittery garrisons was recorded, in 1720, no Mitchell Garrison was listed. When, however, the 1722 list appeared, among the houses ordered to be fortified was that of Joseph Mitchell with the provision "...that ye Inhabitants & familys from Joseph Billings to John Whitney Inclusively Lodge therein."[60] Here we encounter a problem. Was the Joseph Mitchell mentioned here the returned captive or his nephew Joseph Mitchell, son of Richard and Sarah (Couch) Mitchell? It would appear to be the nephew for Mitchell Garrison appears first in the family of the nephew.

Our first problem is followed by a second problem of equal difficulty. When the estate of Richard Mitchell was divided, a plan (1759) of the property was made,[61] which shows a building that is very likely Mitchell Garrison. What is puzzling is that the building on the plan was assigned in the division of the estate to Richard's son, William, rather than to Richard's son, Joseph, who later owned Mitchell

59 For an account of the Mitchell family, see Stackpole, *Old Kittery and Her Families*, pp. 609-616.
60 Stackpole, *Old Kittery and Her Families*, p. 182.
61 York County Probate Records, Estate No. 13292.

Garrison. Perhaps a more comprehensive survey of the York County records would reveal the transfer of this building to Joseph. Joseph Mitchell and his wife, Isabella Bragdon of York, lived in Mitchell Garrison. Joseph was a shipwright and left a fairly sizeable estate. When he died, in 1768, Mitchell Garrison was to be held by his two sons, John and Jeremiah, mariners, of Kittery according to Joseph's will.[62] Eventually, Jeremiah must have gained full title to this property, containing at that time 118 acres, for his only son Joseph received it with the provision that he should pay to his five sisters, Mary, Eunice, Sarah, Hannah, and Lucy, 22 pounds, 18 shillings, 3 pence and 1-3 of a penny each.[63] Joseph Mitchell moved to Waterville, Maine, and sold the garrison to Thomas Grant Sr.

In 1811, Thomas Grant, a carpenter of Kittery, probably a native of York,[64] for $2000 purchased Mitchell Garrison of Joseph and Dorothy Blaisdell Mitchell of Waterville, Maine. The burial ground at Mitchell Garrison contains the graves of Thomas Grant and his two wives, their sister Miss Mary Gunnison, a nurse of Boston, Thomas Grant Jr., Jeremiah Mitchell, and many graves marked by fieldstones without inscription or with inscriptions now illegible. The forest has surrounded this plot and is rapidly encroaching upon it.

Only two of Thomas Grant's four children survived him, Joanna and Thomas. Joanna married Ezra Mitchell of Waterville, Maine, and lived in Orono for some time. Thomas Grant Jr. never married. He lived at Mitchell Garrison and was heir to most of his father's property. When Thomas Jr. died, the farm was valued at $4085, while the full estate was valued at $6277.37.[65] His sole heir was his nephew, Charles A. Mitchell of Minot, Maine.

When Thomas Grant Jr. died, Mr. Mitchell came to his ancestral home and lived for a while at the Hotel Rockingham in Portsmouth and later at Mitchell Garrison, Kittery. He repurchased some land which had been sold from the estate. In 1919, his daughter and sole heir sold Mitchell Garrison. During most of the time after 1919, it was unoccupied till it was purchased in 1937 by Col. Biddle of Cynwyd.

Directly before Mitchell Garrison lies the head of Braveboat Harbor Creek. From the garrison, a few years ago, one could trace the

---

[62] *Ibid*, Estate No. 13277.
[63] *Ibid*, Estate No. 13267.
[64] Thomas Grant was the son of Joseph Grant, a well-to-do farmer, who left extensive property holdings in York, Maine, where the family had resided for many generations. Thomas Grant's successive wives were sisters, Betsey and Sarah Gunnison of Kittery.
[65] *York County Probate Records*, Estate no. 13267.

windings of this creek till it reached the harbor and entered the sea beyond. For years the place has received no care and now the view of the ocean is cut off by a heavy growth of trees. Nature has reclaimed the land that was wrested from her by Mitchells many generations ago. Only occasional fruit trees, brilliant in the bloom of spring, standing amidst pine and hemlock, show where once lay orchards and fields.

THE FORT

Forts in colonial America range in type from the small block-house found (in replica) on Roanoke Island, North Carolina, erected by Raleigh (1584) to the elaborate European fortification, Castillo de San Marcos, erected by the Spanish at St. Augustine, Florida, in 1672, now a national monument.

On Portsmouth Harbor are two forts, both dating from early times, Fort McClary at Kittery Point, and Fort Constitution, formerly Fort William and Mary, at New Castle, New Hampshire. Fort William and Mary was built on the site of a battery which had been erected in that location as early as 1632. Fort William and Mary has gained greater distinction than Fort McClary for it was there the first struggle of the American Revolution occurred Dec. 14-16, 1774, when Langdon and Sullivan led the attack and capture of the fort following Revere's ride to Portsmouth on December 13, 1774.

THE FORT: FORT McCLARY, 1715

Nearly opposite Thaxter Park in a beautiful setting is the present-day entrance of Fort McClary. Driving from York Harbor toward Portsmouth, one passes the park where a pool filled with pond lilies stands before an amphitheatre of forest trees. Bounding the park on the further side is Crockett's Neck Road and next to that the spot at which Spruce Creek, a tidal estuary, borders upon Pepperrell Road. Directly opposite the latter place is an entrance drive to the fort; an opening cut through the woods reveals the blockhouse *(see Fig. 11)*.

On a tree, near the entrance of Fort McClary, is a sign which gives a resume of the fort's history. It reads:

FORT McCLARY

The Province of Massachusetts Bay built a Fort on this site in 1715. Very early it was called Fort William in honor of Sir William Pepperrell. Fort Mc-Clary was established as a military post by the United States in 1812. The Fort was garrisoned during the Revolution and the name changed to Fort McClary in honor of Major Andrew McClary who lost his life in the Battle of Bunker Hill. Fort McClary was rebuilt in 1864. The present granite walls and batteries were constructed at that time. The Fort was purchased by the State of Maine in March, 1924.

The sign tells something of the history of the fort but fails to connect it with the history of the community.

It is difficult to attach a date to the building of Fort McClary. Some historians assert that there are at the fort, four forts built one upon another, 1690, 1721, 1812, and 1864.[66] The answer to this problem depends partly upon one's description of a fort and partly upon what one can read into the early records. There are at least four walls (and possibly five) at Fort McClary built one within another.

In 1715, the Province of Massachusetts Bay voted to build a breast work of six guns at Kittery Point to be maintained by the town; a naval officer for Kittery was determined upon.[67] The reason for this activity, in 1715 (as in 1721), lay in a quarrel between the colonies of Massachusetts and New Hampshire. The colony of New Hampshire had been exacting unreasonable harbor duties and impositions from the Maine province of the Massachusetts Bay Colony. The 1715 fort proved to be a paper fort, for, in 1721, Massachusetts Bay again voted a fort at Kittery Point for the same purpose. There seems to be a strong tradition that the fort was

---

[66] Did the Pepperrells actually have a fort at Kittery Point in 1690? Tradition says they did, but the only support I have found for it is a garrison list of 1690 including Pepperrell's house. Stronger evidence lies in Col. Benjamin Church's mention of "Pepperrell's Fort at Kittery Point," in 1704.
[67] Burrage, *Maine Forts*, pp. 161-189.

called Fort William after Sir William Pepperrell, undoubtedly at a later date for Sir William did not win his fame till 1745. Parsons has asserted that the elder Pepperrell had command of this fort with the rank of captain.[68]

The fort in Kittery was not neglected when the American Revolution came along, as we can see from a resolution passed by the province of Massachusetts Bay:

> RESOLVED, that the Commissary General be and he is hereby directed to deliver to the committee of correspondence, safety and inspection of Kittery aforesaid five hundred pounds weight of gun powder and eighty shot suitable for twelve pounders, and eighty ditto suitable for nine pounders to supply the cannon in the Battery aforesaid for which the said committee or town of Kittery shall be accountable to the General Court.[69]

Possibly because Kittery, New Castle, and Portsmouth were so well defended, they were not attacked. Fort William and Mary at New Castle, across the harbor from Kittery, with Fort McClary, made an excellent defense for the locality.

Mr. Dunnack states that at the time of the Revolutionary War, the name of the fort at Kittery was changed to Fort McClary. Since Major Andrew McClary was sufficiently esteemed by his contemporaries that the Kittery fort was named after him, it seems appropriate that more should be known of his life. Major McClary[70] was a soldier noted for his bravery, good looks, and popularity. He was an inn keeper, town clerk, and large landowner in Epsom, a short distance from Concord, New Hampshire. Like his contemporary, Nathan Hale, he heard the news of Concord and Lexington while engaged in his spring ploughing. He dropped his labor at once, left his wife and seven children, and marched in 24 hours to Cambridge, 70 miles away. Capt. Andrew McClary was unanimously elected as a major in Stark's regiment; he was the highest-ranking American officer to fall at Bunker Hill.

> Having passed the last place of danger, he went back to see if the British were disposed to follow them across the neck, thus exposing himself to danger anew. His men cautioned against his rashness. "The ball is not yet cast that will kill me," said he, when a random shot from one of the frigates struck a buttonwood tree and, glancing, passed through his abdomen. Throwing his hands above his head, he leaped several feet from the ground and fell forward upon his face—dead.[71]

The death of the intrepid major made a profound impression

---

68 Parsons, *Life of Sir William Pepperrell, Bart.*, p. 11.
69 Burrage, *Maine Forts*, p. 173.
70 Biographical information on Majoy McClary is taken from an article on the McClary family by John A. Dolbeer in Hurd, *History of Merrimack and Belknap Counties*, pp. 461-468.
71 Hurd, *History of Merrimack and Belknap Counties*, p. 464.

upon his contemporaries, but today his name is chiefly recalled by a fort in Kittery Point, Maine, named after him.

In 1808, the United States government purchased Fort McClary. During the War of 1812, the government erected fortifications at Fort McClary. The blockhouse may date from 1812, as tradition states, or it may date from the 1840's as some architects feel from the construction of the building.

The War of 1812 occurred so many years ago that we have no personal recollections of the relationship of McClary to that war. With the period intervening between 1812 and the war that commenced in 1861 we do have knowledge of Fort McClary. For some time during this period the keeper of the fort was Col. George Sparhawk. Col. Sparhawk made himself a part of the history of Fort McClary to such an extent that his name is as indelibly associated with the fort in Kittery memories as are the names of Major McClary or 'Squire Bellamy.

Col. Sparhawk, a native of Portsmouth, New Hampshire, was a descendant of a brother of the Sparhawk who married a Pepperrell heiress. The Pepperrell wealth had long since been dissipated when George was a boy, but George's father had inherited the Atkinson fortune of Portsmouth. Though the Atkinson fortune was probably the largest of its time in this section of New England, it did not last long in Sparhawk hands. George came of a family "who though not dissipated, were without business habits, and spent with a thoughtless lavishness that soon made inroads upon a purse which no one made any effort to replenish." In his poverty, as much as in his wealth, George Sparhawk carried with him the air of one much "to the manner born." To an air of personal distinction, he added a sterling character. His obituary notice reads:

> A man of transparent honesty, undoubted integrity, and delicate modesty, in the world of show he never made a great figure, and in his declining days and declining fortunes he made less and less. But in the social circle as a friendly and intelligent companion, and in the domestic as a brother, husband, and father, he had a character which shone brighter and brighter.[72]

Though he tried business many times, George Sparhawk was unsuccessful in a world with different standards than those to which he was accustomed in his way of life. He rose to the rank of Colonel of the First Regiment of the New Hampshire militia, but ill health prevented him from continuing a military career. He secured the appointment of keeper of Fort McClary and there he brought his

72 Sparhawk, *Col. George Sparhawk*. In *Memorial Biographies of the New England Historic Genealogical Society*, v. 3, p. 196.

Scotch-born wife and three daughters to live. At the fort, Col. Sparhawk's wife and one daughter died. Though he lost the appointment of keeper of the fort due to changes in politics, the colonel remained associated with the fort in the minds of his Kittery friends. Wrapped in his great military cloak, he was a familiar figure appearing to his contemporaries to be military and of conspicuous importance though he were fulfilling duties as a clerk at the Navy Yard in Portsmouth, or keeping the books of his friend Robert Follett Gerrish at his Kittery Point warehouse, or teaching school in the old Pepperrell Mansion.

Col. Sparhawk died before the country was rocked with internal war. Once more Fort McClary entered upon a new phase. When the Confederate raider Alabama was reported as seen off Portland, Portsmouth became alarmed. At Kittery Point, the Hon. Charles Gerrish Bellamy of Pepperrell Mansion took the lead in organizing the local defense.

Charles G. Bellamy, a Kittery native son, was a man who made an impression on his time. Someone who spent his youth in Kittery has described Senator Bellamy walking the streets "in true Websterian dignity."[73] Bellamy studied architecture and building construction in Boston. He built the first Kittery Point bridge and many buildings in this vicinity.[74] As one who had served as a Captain in the Maine militia, as Senator in the State Legislature, as Sheriff of York County, and as naval inspector of timber, it seemed appropriate that Bellamy should organize the defense of Kittery in the war. C. G. Bellamy requested of the commanding officer of the U. S. Navy Yard at Portsmouth military supplies; he received cannon, carriages, and ammunition as well as the use of the Navy Yard's chief gunner and his assistant. Senator Bellamy saw his friend Robert Follett Gerrish who agreed to arrange transportation of the guns to the fort. Fifty yoke of oxen were brought in voluntarily by the country farmers to move four of the cannon and carriages. Because it was feared that the Kittery Point bridge was not strong enough, the guns were hauled around Spruce Creek through Kittery Point village. They finally entered the fort close to the point where the casual visitor strolls in today. The cannon were mounted, scaled and fired, but the fort was never challenged. When a single friendly craft was fired upon, the government took over all activity at the fort. Fort McClary became a recruiting station. The most famous recruit at the fort was the noted lawyer who had just retired from the country's

[73] Horace Lunt, in *The Island and Harbor Echo,* v. 4, no. 1 (Jan. 1897), p. 6.
[74] Biographical information on Senator Bellamy (and his connection with Fort McClary) was furnished by his granddaughter, Mrs. Mary Bellamy Safford Wildes.

vice-presidency, the Hon. Hannibal Hamlin, private in Company A, the State Guards.

An enormous granite wall was commenced about the fort. While work was in progress, the war came to a close, and soon all building ceased. Great piles of unused granite lay about. The enlisted men's quarters, the kitchen, the blockhouse, the chapel, the magazine, the hospital, and the guard house were standing in 1870.[75] Thirty-six years later a writer, Herbert Milton Sylvester, visited the fort and left his impressions in writing:

A rude board fence separates it from the highway, over which one climbs to plunge through the tangle of low birch and alder, to come out upon an elevated plateau, where tons of igneous rock have been blasted out of the solid ledge to make way for the granite bastions and angles broken here and there by embrasures for heavy guns which have yet to be mounted. Here is a suggestion of a road, and as one follows it one comes to its extreme easterly scarp, whereby a flight of steps of split stone one reaches the highest level of the work. Here are the magazines and the barracks, and the crazy wooden bridge or steps on the landward side by which one mounts to the doorless entrance of its second story. It is a barren interior, stripped of every vestige of its once familiar appointments. A winding stair leads to the lower regions, where are dog-holes of solid masonry occupying its central area, which may have been intended for the stowing away of ammunition or recalcitrant humanity. Thin ribbons of subdued light came through the numerous slits in the wall... Old Fort M'Clary is a ruin. The government work was long ago abandoned. The old derricks have rotted down. Only the huge piles of split granite and three somewhat heavy ordnance mounted on massive steel carriages indicate the scene of activity that at one time prevailed here.[76]

Today, the fort is even more of a ruin than it was in 1906. The guns have been removed and the buildings, except for the blockhouse, are almost in shambles. The fort is now, however, easily accessible. The ancient blockhouse and the powder magazine have been completely restored. The entire area of approximately twenty-five acres has become a state park. When, in 1922, the U. S. Congress voted to sell some of its old forts, Fort McClary became the property of Maine for the low cost of $3100. Through the efforts of the late Gov. Baxter of Maine, the preservation of Fort McClary is assured. During World War II, Fort McClary became a lookout station for the spotting of enemy planes, but, in 1947, the restoration of the fort, earlier commenced, was to some extent continued.

---

[75] Burrage, *Maine Forts*, p. 175.
[76] Sylvester, *Old York*, pp. 244-245.

THE TAVERN

The tavern played an intimate part in the life of colonial America. Sometimes it was called the inn or the ordinary. It was usually located near the meeting house, a condition sometimes stipulated in the licensing. Sunday often meant a full day of worship in Puritan New England with intermissions during which the worshippers might find food and warmth at the nearby inn.

In the Old World, where water was often poor, beer was a common drink which the New World settler hoped to be able to obtain when possible. Drinking was done only in moderation for there was a severe fine for intemperance. The ordinary was considered to be a necessity, and towns which did not keep one were fined.

Sometimes town meetings were held at the tavern. The submission of Maine to Massachusetts was concluded at the William Everett Tavern in Kittery (now Eliot), in 1652. Not only the tavern was important to the community, but the landlord as well, for he often held positions of trust in the local government.

Among the more notable surviving New England hostelries which have remained taverns are the Wayside Inn, Sudbury, Mass., (1686) and the Wright Tavern, Concord, Mass., (1747).

THE TAVERN: JOAN DEERING HOUSE, 1700

When widow Joan Bray Deering built her Kittery Point house, in 1700, she had been keeping a tavern for five years. She lived for only seven years afterwards though her house for eight years was licensed in her name as a tavern. Considering that this house *(see Fig. 12)* was two hundred forty-seven years old in 1947 and was a tavern for but seven years, it may seem a little odd that the tavern designation should have clung for so many years. After all, Bray House was once a tavern, the Pinkham cottage was once a tavern, even Pepperrell Mansion was for a while a tavern, and yet it is with this house that we associate the tavern. Probably the reason is that Joan Deering built her house as a tavern as well as a dwelling house, whereas the other houses were merely adapted as taverns.

It is not surprising to find Joan Deering keeping a tavern. Her father John Bray was the tavern keeper at the Point for many years, as well as being a shipwright. Her mother-in-law, Widow Deering kept a tavern at first alone and later with her second husband William Crafts at Kittery Point.[77] It was very important that each town should keep a tavern in early New England for the entertainment of the wayfarer, before the innovation of the hotel. When the town did not provide a tavern, often the Court ordered that town to keep one. Joan's father, John Bray, was fined in court for not displaying his tavern sign.[78]

Joan Bray Deering willed her tavern to her only son John Deering, a sea captain. Dr. Stackpole asserts that in 1775, John Deering, grandson of Joan Bray Deering, lived in the tavern.[79] Capt. John Deering had two sons Capt. William Deering and Capt. John Deering Jr. Capt. John Deering Jr. died at sea in 1758, and his family moved to Portland, Maine, where they became wealthy and prominent.[80] Who the John Deering was who had the house, in 1775, I have been unable to discover.

Between 1758 and 1856, we have a gap of almost a hundred years in the history of the Joan Deering house. In 1856, a map of York County, Maine, lists Oliver Cutts as the occupant of this house. In 1864, Oliver sold it to George S. Cutts, who, the following year, sold it to Capt. John Williams. Capt. Williams, and Betsey, his wife, transferred it to their

---

77 For information on the Deering genealogy, see Noyes, *Genealogical Dictionary of Maine and New Hampshire*, pp. 190-192.
78 *Maine Province and Court Records*, v. 2, p. 264.
79 Stackpole, *Old Kittery and Her Families*, p. 60.
80 Deering's Oaks in Portland, and the Portland suburb of Deering, take their names from this family.

son-in-law and daughter, Henry S. and Harriet N. Williams Call. From
the Calls the house passed to the Blaisdells and then to Roscoe E.
Anderson, the present occupant.

Since the Joan Deering house is the only house in Kittery to pass
today under the Deering name, it seems appropriate to relate here the
tragic story of William Deering [81] though the tale by rights belongs to
Bray House where William spent his youth. William Deering was the son
of Capt. Joseph Deering and Margery Bray. His father's brother, Capt.
Clement Deering, was married to his mother's sister, Joan Deering, who
built Deering Tavern. William Deering commanded a vessel engaged in
coastal trade. At the age of twenty-four, he married Mary Pine, daughter
of an Englishman who had come to Marblehead. After the birth of seven
children, when William was forty-one, he murdered his wife. Following
the trial, Deering was condemned to execution. While awaiting execution he was confined in irons in the York Gaol. William must have awak-
ened the sympathy of his cousin Sir William Pepperrell, for Pepperrell
wrote to his friend Gov. Shirley:

> The enclosed is a petition that came to me from the poor condemned prisoner
> in York Gaol which he desired me to forward to your Excellency. I am afraid he is not
> prepared to die, but as you are wise and merciful and know the worth of souls, I
> shall be silent.[82]

Governor Shirley replied seven days later:

> I am favord with yours by last post, inclosing Dearing's petition; and have there-
> upon ordered the secretary to make out a reprieve for him to the – – of September, – –;
> which I hope he will improve, to prepare himself for a better death, than I fear from the
> heinous, unnatural offence for which he is condemned, his life has been. However, I
> shall pay so much further regard to his petition, since he there insinuates that the court
> and jury were deceived by the evidence produced against him, as to inquire into the
> circumstances of it from the judges.[82]

After being twice reprieved by Governor Shirley, no doubt William
Deering became aware that he must swing for his crime. On the night
following September 15th, he escaped from York Gaol. Though he was
freshly pursued he was not recaptured. His escape was attributed to his
cousin Sir William Pepperrell. Sir William must have felt much sympathy for William Deering or he would not have entered so completely
into this stir. I wish we knew more of Deering's later life, but from this
time forward our record is blank.[83] At least we are certain that William

---

[81] Noyes, *Genealogical Dictionary of Maine and New Hampshire*, p. 191.
[82] Parsons, *Life of Sir William Pepperrell, Bart.*, p. 205.
[83] Miss Jessamine Brooks of York Village, curator of the Old York Gaol, has related to me the tradition
that Deering escaped to England on one of the Pepperrell ships which lay in readiness to sail till
Deering had fled the Gaol. See also Banks, *History of York, Maine*, v. 2, p. 244.

Deering was not executed by Massachusetts Bay.

The Joan Deering house is interesting architecturally. The house has a large central chimney. Originally two stories in front and one story in the rear, the house retains its original lines, despite alterations. A dormer addition on the back does not conceal the early proportions. Unfortunately, little of the interior woodwork remains and the small paned lights of glass have been replaced by larger panes.

Though houses have been erected across the road from the Joan Deering house, the old house is on enough of an eminence to preserve its view of the harbor. What scenes the old house has been a silent witness to in the years since 1700! Within full range of the Deering windows the *Ranger* put out to sea with John Paul Jones in command (after she had been built at Badger's Island nearby). Years later came the era of the clipper ship, and the stately *Nightingale*, one of the most beautiful craft ever to grace the ocean, passed the windows of the Deering home on her maiden voyage (after she had been built in Eliot nearby). But a few years after the *Nightingale*, the *Kearsarge* steamed out of Portsmouth Harbor on her maiden voyage (fresh from the Navy's shipyard at Portsmouth) to pursue the Confederate raider *Alabama* to her doom. The close of another war brought Admiral Cervera and the Spanish prisoners into Portsmouth Harbor as prisoners aboard a part of America's battle fleet. The last wars have seen submarine after submarine creep furtively down the harbor prepared to defend American interests and international idealism.

The days of shipping in Portsmouth are gone but the harbor is still filled through the summer. The boats that are there now are pleasure craft which tack around the Fort Foster wharf and Whale's Back Light on pleasant days. Kittery Point still produces men who command ships, among them Capt. Rodney Blake of the U. S. S. *Crown Point.* It is not such a long time since the sea captains sailed from Portsmouth Harbor. As late as 1895, a list[84] of captains from Kittery Point, who sailed down Portsmouth Harbor, included Edwin A. Gerrish, Horace M. Seawards, Charles C. Sawyer, Thomas Amee, Charles W. Frisbee, Berten Hoyt, and junior officers J. Chester Cutts and John H. Pruett.

Many men who sailed out never to return must have been well known to those who lived in Deering Tavern for their deaths touched many homes in Kittery Point. In the 1840's, Capt. Eleazer Williams sailed out of Portsmouth Harbor and was never heard from again. In 1851, Capt. Richard Seaward sailed from Portsmouth Harbor in the schooner *Harvest Home,* bound for the western banks. A few days

---

[84] Capt. C. C. Sawyer in *The Island and Harbor Echo*, v. 4, no. 1 (Jan. 1897), pp. 12-13.

later came a great April gale in which the vessel no doubt foundered with all on board; no trace of her has been found to this day. In 1855, Capt. Smith Amee's ship disappeared (with George Deering aboard). In 1873, Capt. Abraham Deering was lost with all of his crew. In 1880, Capt. Joseph Hunt sailed out of Portsmouth Harbor never to return. All of these men were Kittery Point captains, often with Kittery Point crews. For years and years the sea took a terrific toll from the manhood of this small village.

On a calm summer's day Portsmouth Harbor as seen from Joan Deering's house is peaceful, but on a stormy day one can see the surf thrown high in the air as the waves break against the shaggy rocks of Tavistock Island. It is seldom that ships in distress drift into the harbor though the protruding ribs of a tanker that foundered before Bray House may be seen at low tide. More often ships have foundered on the rocky Isles of Shoals, ten miles out at sea.[85]　The brig *Mary Ellen* was wrecked at Sea Point,[86] and the schooner *Thistle* nearby, while, in 1876, the brig *Hattie Eaton* was wrecked on Gerrish Island near Sea Point with a loss of eight lives. Once a ship has passed Gerrish Island's outer bounds and reached the protection afforded by the reaches of that island and New Castle, she has entered the bounds of security.

[85] For a history of Kittery Point shipwrecks, see the recollections of Benjamin Randall Frisbee, in *The Island and Harbor Echo*, v. 3, no. 1 (Jan. 1896), p. 9.
[86] Sea Point is a part of Cutts Island, Kittery Point.

THE PARSONAGE

Not many homes of the colonial clergy have survived and few of these surviving are without extensive alterations. Often the house has been sold by the church and another house purchased elsewhere or another house erected where the clergyman might live.

Perhaps the finest example extant of the home of a colonial clergyman is the Glebe House (1690) in Woodbury, Connecticut. The Glebe House was the birthplace of the Episcopal Church in America. In the Glebe House, Samuel Seabury was elected the first Episcopal bishop in the United States.

The parsonage at Kittery Point has undergone a considerable amount of renovation and yet has managed to preserve a great many of the old features in the process.

THE PARSONAGE: CONGREGATIONAL CHURCH
PARSONAGE, 1729

The old Congregational Church parsonage, built for the family of Parson Newmarch, in 1729, stands on the grounds of the First Parish Church, with only the new parsonage intervening between the Church and this building where Washington was once entertained *(see Fig. 13)*.

From the street today one sees what appears to be a beautifully preserved colonial structure. The building is enshrouded in lilacs, while above the spreading bushes one catches the gleam of bright sunlight upon panelled window shutters half-closed. Only one room retains the window shutters but the room below it contains a fireplace, a fair amount of panelling and wainscotting, while the stairway is an unusually pleasing specimen of very early American rail and baluster. Unfortunately, a great deal of the interior has been altered but traces of the original woodwork remain in every room.

When the house was built, in 1729, Rev. John Newmarch had for some time labored diligently among his Kittery Point flock. Newmarch[87] was a self-made man, a native of Ipswich, a Harvard graduate, who came to Kittery Point with no means and at first taught school as well as preaching here.

Newmarch, himself, won a warm place in the hearts of his parishioners. The parish was organized, in 1714, when Newmarch was ordained. It grew rapidly and, finally, in 1729, built a house where the pastor might live. During a part of his ministry, Newmarch lived in his own house at Kittery Foreside. He was buried there near the present Newmarch Street; recently his remains have been removed to the parish burial ground. When Newmarch became feeble as he grew older, the parish brought him an assistant; eventually Newmarch retired. The large family of John Newmarch was well educated. When Newmarch died he left an estate worth £5000, with land in other towns than Kittery, and "a surprizing Number of Dollars."

Before Parson Newmarch had been long in his grave, a parish row had broken forth. On Jan. 15, 1754, John Newmarch died. On Feb. 4, 1754, in the *Boston Post Boy* (and on Feb. 11, 1754, in the *Boston Evening Post*), in an obituary notice of the parson, the Newmarch children complained because the Kittery parish had not assisted in their father's burial and because a fee had been charged for the use of the burial

---

[87] For a biography of Newmarch (1672-1754), see Shipton, *Biographical Sketches of Those Who Attended Harvard College in the Classes 1690-1700*, v. 4, pp. 72-75.

cloth. Kittery Point parish was shocked. On March 4, 1754, the parish replied in the *Boston Evening Post* answering the charges. After speaking of how well Newmarch had been treated by the parish throughout his lifetime, it asserted the ingratitude of his family. Once more John and Joseph Newmarch wrote a letter, published in the *Boston Evening Post,* May 13, 1754, in which they savagely berated the Kittery Point parish, and, according to Dr. Shipton, "probably touched the heart of the matter in declaring that as the minister's children they had been treated by envy and hatred, rather than love by the parishioners."[88]

Despite inauspicious beginnings, fire[89] and feud, the Kittery Point parish flourished. Newmarch had planted solidly and Stevens tended carefully. Rev. Benjamin Stevens,[90] the successor of Newmarch, was a scholarly, dignified man. As a boy, son of the Charlestown (Mass.) pastor, Stevens had a close escape from death. A seven-months old infant, when small-pox struck his family, Benjamin was taken from the Charlestown home by a nurse. All who remained in the Charlestown house died, father and mother, two children, sister-in-law, and a maid. Benjamin Stevens was educated at Harvard and married a daughter of Judge Trowbridge of Cambridge. A Harvard alumnus, a gentleman of breeding and distinction, Stevens lived graciously in the old parsonage. Mrs. Stevens died shortly after marriage leaving an only child, Miss Sally (Sarah) Stevens who became the mistress of the house.

Dr. Stevens was an intimate friend of the gentry about Kittery Point, the Barrells of Barrell Grove, the Saywards of Sayward House, the Sewalls of Coventry Hall, the Pepperrells of Pepperrell Mansion, the Sparhawks of Sparhawk Hall, the Hamiltons of Hamilton House. Within this group Dr. Stevens and his daughter Sally were welcome members. A colonial aristocracy had formed at an early date in this section of New England. This class later formed a nucleus of Tory sympathizers in the Maine province of Massachusetts Bay. Only the fear that Dr. Stevens might have loyalist sympathies, prevented his election as president of Harvard College.

A diligent worker, Stevens cared for his Kittery Point flock and his home. His hedged garden, adjacent to the parsonage, was tended

---

88 Shipton, *Biographical Sketches of Those Who Attended Harvard College in the Classes 1690-1700,* v. 4, p. 75.
89 See the First Parish Church, in this book.
90 For a biography of Stevens (1720-1791), see Lee, *Memoirs of Rev. Joseph Buckminster, D.D., and of His Son, Rev. Joseph Stevens Buckminster,* pp. 51-66, and a manuscript on early Kittery Point history by Mrs. S. S. B. Wood, in the library of the New England Historic Genealogical Society, in Boston.

by his colored servant. The parsonage was well furnished, its walls adorned by many portraits including one of Mrs. Stevens which hung above a fireplace mantel. Mrs. Sarah Sayward Barrell Wood (Maine's first novelist) has mentioned the time as a girl she visited the Stevens' at the parsonage. She says: "I thought it the most delightful place I had ever seen."[91] Fortunately for Dr. Stevens, his daughter did not go far from him when she married. She became the wife of the Rev. Dr. Joseph Buckminster, pastor of the North Church in Portsmouth.

Dr. Buckminster's daughter has left an interesting account of Dr. Stevens' life. She relates in it an amusing anecdote of the veneration in which the learning of Dr. Stevens was held by his parishioners:

> The writer, some years ago, met with a singular proof of the whimsical idea Dr. Stevens's parishioners entertained of his great learning. Passing in a small boat over the river to the "Point," an ancient boatman ... sat at the helm, and paddled the boat across. Being asked if he remembered Dr. Stevens, --"Remember him, indeed!" he answered; "he not only baptized, but he married me also." "Ah!" he said, "he was a prodigiously learned man, and never spoke except in Greek and Hebrew."[92]

When Washington visited Portsmouth, in 1789, he was taken on a fishing trip, on the 2nd of November. As the little fishing craft passed the fort at New Castle, Washington was tendered a 13-gun salute. With the president were President (corresponding to the later Governor) John Sullivan of New Hampshire and Senator John Langdon, as well as other gentlemen.[93] The group landed on the Kittery shore and called on Parson Stevens at the parsonage. A few days after Washington's momentous visit, Dr. Stevens' old and dear friend Lady Mary Pepperrell died. The following year, the doctor's daughter Sally died, and within a few months the doctor followed Sally to the grave. Those who knew the doctor intimately said he was never the same after the death of his child.[94]

There are so many stories and traditions about Dr. Stevens that it is impossible to repeat them here. On cold and stormy winter Sundays, in his old age, Dr. Stevens[95] would send his servant, black Sambo, to the meeting house to see how many persons were in attendance. If there were seven or less, they were invited to the parsonage and the service conducted in the library. If there were more than seven, Dr. Stevens went to the Church. Dr. Stevens was

---

91 Wood MS, New England Historic Genealogical Society, Boston.
92 Lee, *Memoirs of Rev. Joseph Buckminster, D.D., and of His Son, Rev. Joseph Stevens Buckminster*, p. 56.
93 Decatur, *Private Affairs of George Washington*, p. 35.
94 Lee, *Memoirs of Rev. Joseph Buckminster, D.D., and of His Son, Rev. Joseph Stevens Buckminster*, p. 61.
95 *Ibid*, p. 54.

one of the founders of the Piscataqua Association of Ministers. When he died, he left his library for the use of the clergy of the surrounding towns, a circulating library. It was one of the earliest libraries of this type in existence. The books were kept at the parsonage where a considerable number of them remain.

The next incumbent of the Kittery Point parish, the Rev. Jonas Hartwell was the son-in-law of Capt. Samuel Smallcorn, owner of Pepperrell Mansion. Jonas and Sally, his wife, do not seem to have been happy here. Perhaps it was a difficult task to follow after Benjamin Stevens. Jonas commenced to drink heavily;[96] after six years he was requested to resign. Jonas and his family moved "down East" in Maine, where he died; later the parish at Kittery Point assisted in the support of his family.

Following Jonas Hartwell came the Rev. William Briggs. Like Mr. Hartwell, Mr. Briggs kept few parish records and we have only vacancies in the parish registers. During Mr. Briggs' incumbency, we are told that the parish reached its lowest ebb when only one member was in attendance at services, Mrs. Tamsen Haley Bellamy.[97] Hearing that Mr. Briggs was considering selling the church communion service to obtain support, Mrs. Bellamy arranged to have the communion service smuggled from the church and taken by night to the Gerrish Island home of Col. Joseph Gerrish who was interested in the church. At Col. Gerrish's house the silver remained secreted over several years but was returned by him to the parish after Mr. Briggs had left.

The church had fallen upon evil days and was finally closed for six years. It was revived through the efforts of the Rev. Tobias Ham Miller[98] of Portsmouth. Mr. Miller was a printer, a native of Portsmouth. After working for a while on the *Newburyport Herald,* he became joint proprietor and associate editor of the *Portsmouth Chronicle.* He studied for the ministry with his friend the Rev. Samuel W. Clarke of Greenland, and, in 1836, was licensed to preach by the Piscataqua Association of Ministers. He was commissioned a missionary to the eastern part of New Hampshire as well as pastor of the Kittery Point parish. Ordained a pastor in 1837, he was dismissed by the association when he became a Universalist. Mr. Miller founded the Universalist Church in Portsmouth. During his ministry at

---

96 *Old Eliot,* v. 5, no. 1 (Jan. 1902), p. 53.
97 Recollections of a descendant, Mrs. Mary Bellamy Safford Wildes.
98 Biographical data on the Rev. T. H. Miller (1801-1870) was taken from manuscript notes owned by a descendant, Mrs. Fred Drake of Portsmouth, N. H.

Kittery Point, the little church had been repaired and rededicated.

With few exceptions, the First Parish Church has remained open and supplied with clergy since the time of Mr. Miller. For many years it was served by young clergymen and was one of the standard "early charges." In later years, it has been served by more elderly men as Mr. Graham, Mr. Newcomb, and Mr. McDonald, the present incumbent. The church is as large at the present time as it has been at any time in its history since the early divisions of the parish were made.

Elder Graham,[99] an Englishman by birth, came to Kittery Point at the age of sixty-one after serving parishes in Maine, New Hampshire, Vermont, and Massachusetts. He died while pastor at Kittery Point. Several of his daughters have made the Kittery vicinity their home. The Rev. Edward H. Newcomb closely identified himself with the village life at Kittery Point and served for a number of years as president of the Kittery Historical Society, as well as being one of its charter members. Mr. McDonald, who arrived in 1947, came to Kittery Point from Westbrook, Maine.

In 1909,[100] a new parsonage was built when the old parsonage had reached a state of disrepair. For some time the old parsonage was fast advancing toward dilapidation. Finally, a bequest made by the Rev. John Sewall, D.D. provided for the renovation of the building; it was named the Benjamin Stevens Community House. Additions to the rear of the building housing a modern kitchen and a stage were made under Mr. Graham and Mr. Newcomb. The building is the meeting place of all parish activities, and the Kittery Historical Society. It serves today a vital place in the community life.

---

[99] Biographical information on the Rev. John Graham (1859-1931) was taken from the *Congregational Year Book* (1931), p. 52.
[100] Information supplied by Agnes Graham Cutts (Mrs. Joseph W. Cutts).

THE CHURCH

The oldest church in the United States is located on Jamestown Island, Virginia. The original tower was erected in 1639, but the remainder of the church is a restoration. The Jamestown Church is used for special services. Another building erected by the Church of England, St. Luke's Church, Smithfield, Va., around 1650, is the oldest church in the United States which has been continually used for worship.

Both the Jamestown Church and St. Luke's, Smithfield, were stone churches. In New England few, if any, stone churches were built in early times. The usual church buildings in New England are of wood, like the church at Kittery Point. These churches were painted white; they are austere and dignified, often graced by beautiful spires.

THE CHURCH: FIRST PARISH CHURCH, 1730

During the 1947 tercentenary celebration in Kittery, the earliest record book of the First Parish Church was placed on exhibition, for perhaps the first time in its history; this record book is preserved in a bank vault as are also the burial pall and the communion silver.

The parish church at Kittery Point is a Congregational Church, served during its early years by clergymen educated at Harvard in the traditions of Massachusetts Bay theology common to that time. As early as 1653, there were probably religious services held at Kittery Point, antedating the present building by almost a century. By 1669,[101] Kittery decided to build a new meeting house at the Point replacing "the old meeting house," on the same spot where the old one then stood. That a new meeting house was needed, that the meeting house then used should be called old would indicate that the meeting house had been there for some time.

When, in 1671, a meeting house was built in the northern part of Kittery, the residents of the southern part (or Kittery Point area) were ordered to return to those living in the northern part whatever monies had been paid by them toward the building of the new meeting house. In 1695, the First Parish Church building was repaired. In 1727, a third building was erected at the Point but it was struck by lightning and destroyed by the ensuing fire. A fourth structure followed, the building standing today *(see Fig. 14)*.

The exterior of the First Parish Church has been partially altered. Originally this building had a tall belfry and faced toward the west; it was located where Pepperrell Road runs today. In 1874, the building was repaired, moved about sixty feet northward, and turned south. A tradition states that the frame of the meeting house was hewn somewhere about Dover and floated down the stream.[102]

The interior of this building *(see Fig. 15)*, though it was restored in 1904, still is not the same as when originally built. The pulpit was in the center of one side of the church. Galleries ran about three sides of the building. Only one of the three galleries now remains. In 1904, the pulpit which was completely removed in 1874 was taken from a nearby barn and returned as well as the two panelled box pews at the front of the church. The two front pews were reserved for the gentry as they still are in some of the English country churches. Very likely, as in old England, some member of the gentry, rather than the clergyman, read the scripture

---

[101] Data on the church is given in Stackpole, *Old Kittery and Her Families*, pp. 183-192, and an article by Mrs. Constance Billings, in the *Portsmouth Herald*, June 21, 1947.
[102] Drake, *Nooks and Corners of the New England Coast*, p. 142.

lesson. One of the box pews now holds the console of the pipe organ, while the other, the box pew of Sir William Pepperrell, looks much as it must have looked when built. Unlike other pews in the church, the Pepperrell pew was cushioned, an unusual concession in a Puritan parish. The Pepperrell pew is today occupied by the family of John Mead Howells, distinguished architect and author; it was formerly occupied by his father, the late William Dean Howells.

The communion silver consists of six beakers, a baptismal basin and a tankard, in each case, save for the tankard, appropriately inscribed with the donor's name. The baptismal basin was the work of Samuel Minott of Boston; three of the beakers were the work of William Whittemore of Portsmouth, son of Sir William Pepperrell's sister Margery. The greater part of the silver was the gift of the Pepperrell family. The Pepperrells were a devout family, much attached to the church. Sir William Pepperrell's eldest sister, Mary, after the death of her first husband, was twice married to clergymen. Her youngest sister Jane married a clergyman, her third husband. Pepperrell's sister Dorothy married the son of Parson Newmarch of Kittery Point. Sir William's niece, Sarah Frost, was the wife of the pastor at Newcastle. His wife, Lady Pepperrell, was sister-in-law of two Boston clergymen, while among the Pepperrell descendants there has been a vast number of clergy. One piece of silver belonging to the communion service of this parish was the gift of Jane Pepperrell, wife of the Rev. Ebenezer Tirrell of Medford, Mass. The sole piece of silver not given by the Pepperrell family is that given by William Whipple of Whipple Garrison, Kittery, father of Gen. William Whipple, a signer of the Declaration of Independence, who was christened in this church. Whipple silver, donated in 1728, is the oldest silver owned by the parish.

The burial pal[103] placed on exhibition at the parish house during the 1947 tercentenary was the same that draped the coffin of Sir William Pepperrell in 1745. It was last used in fulfilment of an expressed request, in 1942, at the interment of James H. Walker, for many years clerk of this parish and one who loved and studied its history.

The bell of this church dates from 1714. Capt. Stephen Eastwick, a sea captain, whose father Dr. Pheasant Eastwick, had settled in Portsmouth, gave one half the cost of the bell in return for the privilege of building himself a pew. All others who built pews were required to pay five pounds. The fire of 1729 ruined the bell and it was recast being sent

103 The parish owns another pall for the burial of children; it matches the larger pall and is said to date from the same time.

to London in one of Col. Pepperrell's ships for this purpose. Apparently, this recasting was not successful for, in 1742, it was recast at the expense of Sir William Pepperrell. The latest recasting of this bell took place after the Revolution when it was recast in the iron works founded by Paul Revere. At the present time, the bell is cracked and needs a new casting. In 1714, nineteen males and twenty-five females subscribed to the covenant at this parish. Perhaps some of them are buried in the little churchyard across the road from the church, though I have found but eleven graves there dating from the eighteenth century: John Morse, 1741; John Walker, 1743; Thomas Jenkins, 1745; John Newmarch, 1754;[104] Nicholas Eve, 1759; Robert Cutt Whipple, 1761; Mary Stevens, 1763; Capt. Robert Follett, 1780; Benjamin Stevens, 1791; Mary Chauncey Cutts, 1795; and Mary Follett, 1797. Robert Cutt Whipple was brother to the signer of the Declaration of Independence mentioned earlier.

The parish burial ground is a fascinating place in which to wander. It was fenced by a parish vote in 1733. Here are interred some of Kittery's first families, Cutts, Raynes, Gerrish and Follett. The inscription on the stone of the Hon. James W. Remick is worth recording for it expresses what many have felt who have been buried here. Judge Remick,[105] who was arbiter of U. S. claims after World War I, was a native of Hardwick, Vermont. He made his home at Sunshine Hill on Crockett's Neck Road, Kittery Point. Judge Remick was for some time president of the Kittery Historical Society. His epitaph reads:

I have chosen to have my ashes placed here because I revere this ancient cemetery and the historic church across the way by which it is governed. And I have selected the rough boulder which marks this spot because it was found imbedded in the trail leading through the woods on my own Sunshine Hill, where I have passed so many happy years, and because my dog Teddy and I have walked it so often. James W. Remick, 1860-1943.

There are many interesting epitaphs in this old cemetery. Perhaps the most delightful of all is that on the stone of Nicholas Eve, a quaint rough looking stone; it reads simply: "Old and Still." On the stone of Margaret Hills[106] is found the epitaph:

I lost my life on the raging seas
A sovereign God does as he please;
The Kittery friends they did appear
And my remains they buried here.

---

104 The remains of the Rev. John Newmarch, together with the remains of his wife and child, were removed to this burial ground, Aug. 30, 1936.
105 For a biography of James Waldron Remick, see *Who's Who in America*, v. 14 (1926-27), p. 1598. See also Remick, *Writings, Speeches, Experiences and Philosophy of James W. Remick*, Rumford Press, Concord, N. H. 1934.
106 Margaret, wife of Oliver Hills, was drowned in 1803, aged 28 years.

The stone of Moses McClintock (1814) has a slight variation of an old theme:

> Behold all men as you pass by,
> As you are now, so once was I;
> As I am now, so must you be,
> Prepare for death and follow me.

The epitaph of Elizabeth Fernald (1816) reads simply:

> By my request
> Let this dust rest.

An interesting epitaph is that written by Robert Browning for a leading American interpreter, Levi Lincoln Thaxter. Mr. Thaxter was husband of the noted poetess Celia Thaxter (who is buried at the Isles of Shoals) and father of the well-known botanist and Harvard professor Roland Thaxter, who is buried nearby. The Browning epitaph, written by request of Roland Thaxter, is carved on the stone. The lettering is illegible, but, in 1947, Miss Rosamond Thaxter of Champernowne Farm, Kittery Point, had a bronze marker placed on the irregular boulder brought from Cutts Island marking the grave. The epitaph reads:

> Thou, whom these eyes saw never! Say friends true
> Who say my soul, helped onward by my song,
> Though all unwittingly, has helped thee too?:
> I gave of but the little that I knew:
> How were the gift requited, while along
> Life's path I pace, couldst thou make weakness strong!
> Help me with knowledge—or Life's Old-Death's New!
>
> R. B. to L. L. T., April 1885.

The parish burial ground is rough, irregular, overgrown but not at all displeasing. Little paths have been worn by pilgrims to some of the most interesting spots in the yard, among them the graves of the unknown sailors who lost their lives in the wreck of the brig *Hattie Eaton* on Gerrish Island.

One of the most pleasant spots has not been frequented by visitors. It is a single grave, somewhat away from the others and hidden at almost every viewpoint within the cemetery from the wanderer. A slight knoll conceals this grave which looks down over Lawrence Cove where Robert Cutts built his ships and across to the site of Alexander Shapleigh's house, the first building in Kittery Point.[107] From little Charles

---

[107] Shapleigh's home was located near the present summer cottage of Mrs. Decatur Wright of Chestnut Hill, Pennsylvania.

Hagner's grave, one can see the site of William Crafts' inn where he was directed by the court to provide beer, victuals and cakes for the persons who attended divine worship. I do not know who Charles Hagner was, for Hagner is not a Kittery Point name. Not just the location of the grave is attractive. The lot must have once been beautiful for it is surrounded by a delicate iron fence. Unfortunately, time has not dealt kindly with it and the iron fence has bent almost to the ground, while the turnstile has so rusted that it will not move. One simply steps across the fence into a mass of wild foliage half as high as the miniature obelisk that marks the single grave. One side of the stone reads, Charles Francis Hagner, the other reads, A lamb of the first year without blemish.

EPILOGUE

In 1871, a small funeral procession wended its way along Pepperrell Road from St. John's Church in Portsmouth. It passed the old parsonage, the Lady Pepperrell House, the parish church and Fort McClary. When it reached Pepperrell Mansion, it turned left along the driveway to the tomb of the Pepperrells. The casket that contained the remains of the last of Sir William's grandchildren to be buried here was moved by the bearers toward the mound. The action paused for the brief service of committal.

The warm afternoon sun of late August streamed through the circular opening about the tomb; the cool breeze from the Atlantic stirred the pine tree branches. Beneath the trees the small group waited; only the voices of the clergy and the sound of the wind in the branches was heard. Dr. Davies read from The Book of Common Prayer:

Most merciful Father, who hast been pleased to take unto thyself the soul of this thy servant; Grant to us who are still in our pilgrimage, and who walk as yet by faith, that having served thee with constancy on earth, we may be joined hereafter ... in glory everlasting ... [108]

The death of Miss Sparhawk marked the passing of an era in Kittery Point. Her ninety years reached back into the days when Kittery Point was almost a Pepperrell fief. There were few persons living who could remember that time.

The rise of the machine age had brought with it new manners, new attitudes. The genteel living that Miss Sparhawk enjoyed would soon

---

[108] *The Book of Common Prayer*, p. 336.

become an economic and social impossibility. The intervening years had brought many changes, not only new ideas but new faces, new names. There were people living in Kittery Point who did not even know of the existence of the old lady across the harbor.

Only a few years before Harriet died, the door of the tomb gave way. It soon became popular sport for small boys to play in the tomb. With lighted candle, a group would advance to the center of the structure. Someone of the boys would blow out the candle and shriek out into the darkness: "Old Pepperrell's coming— old Pepperrell's coming!" With wild scampering the boys would rush forth from the tomb. Someone who was present counted the bodies; there were twenty-nine at the time.[109] When Miss Sparhawk heard of the dilapidation of the tomb, she had a crypt built at one side with all of the bodies placed in it, and the tomb sealed again.

In Kittery Point the buildings and their surroundings remind us of those who once loved them. The locality is hallowed by association and message. Kittery Point still echoes the footfall of Sally Cutts and George Sparhawk.

Sarah Orne Jewett wrote of Miss Sally Chauncey Cutts who had passed through domestic tragedy and insanity:

Poor creature! It was a blessed thing that her shattered reason made her unconscious of the change in her fortunes, and incapable of comparing the end of her life with its beginning. To herself, she was still Miss Chauncey, a gentlewoman of high family, possessed of unusual worldly advantages. The remembrance of her cruel trials and sorrows had faded from her mind. She had no idea of the poverty of her surroundings when she paced back and forth, with stately steps, on the ruined terraces of her garden; the ranks of lilies and the conserve-roses were still in bloom for her, and the box-borders were as trimly kept as ever...The twilight had closed round her gradually, and she was alone in her house, but she did not heed the ruin of it or the absence of her friends. On the morrow, life would go on again.[110]

Though Miss Sally was mentally deranged, the patterns of activity she followed were so vivid that they impress us today.

---

109 Hawes, *Some Haunted Houses and Their Ghosts.* In the Lewiston Journal, August 5, 1916.
110 Jewett, *Deephaven*, p. 237.

When Sally Cutts was a young woman, George Sparhawk died, but they must have known one another well. Though Col. Sparhawk was not seen by anyone now living, he seems vital because what he believed is vital today. A relative of the colonel's wrote of him:

The middle of November, 1857, in a little house at Kittery, Maine, a man lay dying...It was an uneventful life that was drawing to its close with this November day. It had been no beacon light to men, but like a cheerful hearth-fire it had comforted many with its genial warmth, and many remember how sparkles and flashes of wit enlivened its steady glow. Mr. Sparhawk had wit and some literary ability; but possessing many desirable faculties, he lacked the money-making one, and this lack, together with years of ill-health, brought him some privations. But he had a hopeful temperament and an unshaken faith in God, and the relatives and friends who watched at his bedside learned not to regret the days of loneliness and pain in his life when they saw how faith and joy held possession of him.[111]

---

[111] Sparhawk, *Col. George Sparhawk.* In *Memorial Biographies of the New England Historic Genealogical Society,* pp. 195-6.

Figure 1. Bray House. *(pp. 9, 83)*

Figure 2. First Parish Church (now First Congregational Church) with the Lady Pepperrell House in the background. *(pp. 14, 84)*

Figure 3. Lady Pepperrell House. *(pp. 14, 84)*

Figure 4. Lady Pepperrell House interior. *(pp. 14, 84)*

Figure 5. Sir William Pepperrell Mansion. *(pp. 22, 85)*

Figure 6. Sir William Pepperrell Mansion, interior. *(pp. 22, 85)*

Figure 7. Counting House and Bellamy workshop. *(pp. 25, 66, 92)*

Figure 8. Sparhawk Hall. *(pp. 27, 86)*

Figure 9. Sparhawk Hall, interior. *(pp. 27, 86)*

Figure 10. Mitchell Garrison. *(pp. 34, 87)*

Figure 11. Fort McClary. *(pp. 39, 88)*

Figure 12. Joan Deering House. *(pp. 45, 88)*

Figure 13. Old Parsonage. *(pp. 50, 89)*

Figure 14. First Parish Church (Congregational Church). *(pp. 56, 90)*

Figure 15. First Parish Church (Congregational Church), interior. *(pp. 56, 90)*

Figure 16. Major Cutts store. *(pp. 66, 91)*

Figure 17. Gerrish Warehouse and Gerrish House. *(pp. 68, 93)*

Figure 18. Gerrish Warehouse hoist. *(pp. 68, 93)*

Figure 19. 1798 House. *(pp. 70, 96)*

Figure 20. The 1763 House (A.K.A. Frizzell-Phillips House. *(pp. 70, 97)*

Figure 21. Kerswell Ordinary. *(pp. 70, 97)*

Figure 22. Champernowne Farm, built on the site of Cutts House. *(pp. 72, 99)*

Figure 23. Willowbank. *(pp. 76, 102)*

Figure 24. Samuel Badger House. *(pp. 76, 103)*

Figure 25. Dennett House. *(pp. 78, 104)*

Figure 26. Dennett House, interior. *(pp. 79, 104)*

Figure 27. Shapleigh House, rear. *(pp. 79, 105)*

Figure 28. Dodovah Curtis House. *(pp. 80, 105)*

BIBLIOGRAPHY

BILLINGS, CONSTANCE (MRS. EVERETT BILLINGS). A series of articles on Kittery Point buildings published in the *Portsmouth Herald*, May 24-July 19, 1947.
285-Year Old John Bray House in Kittery Point Harbors Rich Portion of Kittery's History. May 24, 1947.
William Pepperrell Mansion, Kittery Point, Restored by Owner. May 31, 1947.
Lady Pepperrell Mansion in Kittery Point Survives Years, Fire to Join Celebration. June 7, 1947.
Sparhawk Mansion in Kittery Point Built in 1742 as Wedding Gift for Pepperrell Girl. June 14, 1947.
Kittery Point Church Built in 1730 Becomes Old Landmark. June 21, 1947.
Kittery Point Parsonage 218 Years Old. June 28, 1947.
Old Dennett House Built of Solid Logs. July 5, 1947.
Open House Day July 24 Starts Kittery's Tercentenary Festival. July 6, 1947.
Howells Library, Benson Studio to Open. July 12, 1947.
Old Gerrish House at Kittery Point Dates Back to 1700. July 19, 1947.
Biographical Review. York County, Maine. Boston. Biographical Review Publishing Company. 1896.
BREWSTER, CHARLES WILLIAM. *Rambles About Portsmouth.* First series. Portsmouth. C. W. Brewster and Son. 1859. Second series. Portsmouth. Lewis W. Brewster. 1869.
BROWN, JOHN H., JR. *Portsmouth Navy Yard 1800- and Her Early Commandants.* New York. The Newcomen Society of England. 1947.
CHAPLIN, LEOLA BOWIE. *The Life and Works of Nathaniel Deering.* Orono. University of Maine. 1934.
CLAYTON, W. WOODFORD. *History of York County, Maine.* Philadelphia. Everts and Peck. 1880.
Congregational Year Book. 1879-1922. Boston. Congregational Publishing Society. 1879-1922.
DECATUR, STEPHEN, JR. *Private Affairs of George Washington from the Records and Accounts of Tobias Lear Esquire His Secretary.* Boston. Houghton, Mifflin Company. 1933.
DENNETT, ALEXANDER. *Kittery Ancient and Modern.* Kittery. Kittery Community Service Association. 1925.
DRAKE, SAMUEL ADAMS. *Nooks and Corners of the New England Coast.* New York. Harper and Brothers. 1875.
DRUMMOND, JOSIAH HAYDEN. *John Bray of Kittery.* In *Maine Historic Genealogical Recorder*, v. 3, no. 4 (1886), pp. 248-256, and v. 4, no. 1 (1887), pp. 25-28.
DUNNACK, HENRY ERNEST. *Maine Forts.* Augusta. Press of Charles E. Nash and Son. 1924.
EMERY, WILLIAM MORRELL. *Newell Ancestry. The Story of the Antecedents of William Stark Newell.* (privately printed) 1944.

FERNALD, MARK. *Life of Elder Mark Fernald.* Newburyport. George Moore Payne and D. F. Pike. 1852.

GOOLD, WILLIAM. *The Burning of Falmouth (Now Portland) Maine, by a British Squadron, in 1778.* In the *New England Historical and Genealogical Register,* v. 27, no. 3 (July 1873), pp. 256-266.

GUNNISON, GEORGE W. *A Genealogy of the Descendants of Hugh Gunnison of Boston, Massachusetts 1610-1876.* Boston. George A. Foxcroft. 1880.

HAWES, ANNIE M. L. Some Haunted Houses and Their Ghosts. In the *Lewiston Journal, Illustrated Magazine Section,* Aug. 5, Aug. 12, 1916.

HILL, NOLA. *Bellamy's Greatest Eagle.* In *Antiques,* v. 51, no. 4 (Apr. 1947), p. 259.

HOWARD, CECIL HAMPDEN CUTTS. *Genealogy of the Cutts Family in America.* Albany. J. Munsell's Sons. 1892.

Materials for a Genealogy of the Sparhawk Family in New England. Salem. The Salem Press. 1892.

The Pepperrells in America. Salem. Essex Institute. 1906.

HOWELLS, JOHN MEAD. *The Architectural Heritage of the Piscataqua.* New York. Architectural Book Publishing Company, Inc. 1937.

HUMPHREYS, FREDERICK. *The Humphreys Family in America.* New York. Humphreys Print. 1883.

HURD, D. HAMILTON, *ed. History of Merrimack and Belknap Counties, New Hampshire.* Philadelphia. J. W. Lewis and Company. 1885.

Island and Harbor Alumni Association. *The Island and Harbor Echo.* Kittery Point. Island and Harbor Alumni Association, v. 2, no. 1 (Jan. 1896); v. 4, no. 1 (Jan. 1897).

JEWETT, SARAH ORNE. *Deephaven.* Boston. Houghton Mifflin Company. 1877.

Jones, Edward Alfred. *The Loyalists of Massachusetts.* London. The Saint Catherine Press. 1930.

LEE, ELIZA BUCKMINSTER. *Memoirs of Rev. Joseph Buckminster, D. D., and of His Son, Rev. Joseph Stevens Buckminster.* Boston. William Crosby and H.P. Nichols. 1849.

Maine Historical Society. *Province and Court Records of Maine.* 3 vols. Portland. Maine Historical Society. 1928-1947.

NASON, EMMA HUNTINGTON. *Old Colonial Houses in Maine.* Maine Society of Colonial Dames. Augusta. 1908.

NETTELS, CURTIS PUTNAM. *The Roots of American Civilization.* New York. F. S. Crofts and Company. 1946.

NOYES, SYBIL, CHARLES THORNTON LIBBY AND WALTER GOODWIN DAVIS. *Genealogical Dictionary of Maine and New Hampshire.* Portland. The Southworth-Anthoensen Press. 1928-1939.

PENROSE, CHARLES. *Old Kittery Land of Adventure 1647 —and Captain Francis Champernowne.* New York. The Newcomen Society of England. 1947.

REMICK, OLIVER PHILBRICK. *A Record of the Services of the Commissioned Officers and Enlisted Men of Kittery and Eliot, Maine Who Served Their Coun-*

try on Land and Sea in the American Revolution from 1775 to 1783. Boston. A. Mudge and Son. 1901.

RICHARDSON, HARRIET TABER. J*ohn Bray House in Kittery, Maine*. In *House Beautiful*, v. 65, no. 5 (May 1929), pp. 704-712.

SAFFORD, MOSES ATWOOD. *Historic Homes of Kittery*. In *Collections of the Maine Historical Society*, series 2, v. 5 (1895), pp. 113-128, 387-407.

SAFFORD, VICTOR. *The Woodcarver of Kittery Point*. In *Antiques*, v. 27, no. 3 (Mar. 1935), pp. 102-107.

SALTONSTALL, WILLIAM GURDON. *Ports of Piscataqua*. Cambridge, Mass. Harvard University Press. 1941.

SEWALL, SAMUEL. T*he Diary of Samuel Sewall*. In *Massachusetts Historical Society Collections,* 5th series, v. 5 (Boston. Massachusetts Historical Society. 1878); v. 6 (Boston. Massachusetts Historical Society. 1879); v. 7 (Boston. Massachusetts Historical Society. 1882).

SHIPTON, CLIFFORD KENYON. *Biographical Sketches of Those Who Attended Harvard College in the Classes 1690-1700*. Sibley's Harvard Graduates. Cambridge. Harvard University Press. v. 4, 1933, v. 7 (published by Massachusetts Historical Society) 1945.

SPARHAWK, (MISS) FRANCES CAMPBELL. *Col. George Sparhawk*. In *Memorial Biographies of the New England Historic Genealogical Society*, v. 3. Boston. New England Historic Genealogical Society. 1883.

STACKPOLE, EVERETT SCHERMERHORN. *Old Kittery and Her Families*. Lewiston, Me. The Lewiston Journal Company. 1903.

STEVENS, JOHN AUSTIN. *The First American Baronet*. In *The Magazine of American History*, v. 2 (1878), pp. 673-684.

SYLVESTER, HERBERT MILTON. *Old York*. Boston. W. B. Clarke Company. 1909.

Three Hundredth Anniversary Publications Committee. *Old Kittery 1647-1947*. Kittery. Three Hundredth Anniversary Publications Committee. 1947.

Who's Who in America. 24 vols. Chicago. The A. N. Marquis Company. 1899/1900-

Who's Who in Commerce and Industry. Chicago. The A. N. Marquis Company. 1946.

Who's Who in New England. Chicago. The A. N. Marquis Company.

WILLIS, JOHN LEMUEL MURRAY, *ed. Old Eliot*. 9 vols. Eliot. Augustine Caldwell. 1897-1909.

APPENDIX I

SOME KITTERY POINT BUILDINGS OF
SIGNIFICANT INTEREST

Many of the most interesting buildings of Kittery Point have not been discussed in this work, while some of them have been touched upon and others not mentioned at all. Major Thomas Donnell Cutts who lived at Pepperrell Mansion kept a store nearby. **Major Cutts' store** *(see Fig. 16)* is at the rear of the store of Frisbee Brothers.[112] In 1828, Daniel Frisbee and Solomon Williams purchased the building and commenced a store. The store has been conducted over one hundred twenty years by four generations of Frisbees, Daniel; Solon; Daniel and Frank; Daniel and the son of the late Frank Frisbee. It has passed under three names, the **Daniel Frisbee Store, Solon Frisbee and Company,** and **Frisbee Brothers.**

The Major Cutts store is of curious construction. The high-pitched roof which would seem to indicate early construction is deceptive. The roof line was given its high pitch, in 1828, when Daniel Frisbee doubled the size of the original building. The contrast between the late portion of the building and the early portion may be seen well in the cellar where the old hand-hewn beams are open. On the main floor, the ceiling is low, and the windows at the rear command a view of Portsmouth Harbor. The older part of the building is said to have belonged to the Pepperrells and it may have very well belonged to them for it sits on Pepperrell property. The building is worth noting as it was the store used by George S. Wasson, author and artist, as **Cap'n Simeon's** store in his book by that name.

Another Pepperrell building surviving in part is the old **Pepperrell countinghouse** *(see Fig. 7)* which stands before the site of the Pepperrell wharves. Many of the old timbers may be seen in this building which was remodeled by the wood carver Bellamy and used by him as a carving shop. It has been adapted as a studio cottage and is the residence of Martin Frost. Its history while owned by the Bellamys appears in the chapter on Pepperrell Mansion.

A group of buildings is owned by Charles S. Gerrish of Portsmouth and Kittery Point, including the **Follett residence** and the **Gerrish warehouse**. The Gerrish property is approached by a winding lane shaded by the same trees that shade the parish burial ground. One end of the

---

[112] Information supplied by Daniel Frisbee.

house, according to Mr. Gerrish, was built as early as 1700. The other end was added several years later. In its original state the house was known as the **"Piggin House"**. The name remained with the house for many years though all resemblance to a piggin (a firkin with one stave protruding for a handle) was gone after the single end chimney had become the center chimney. Much of this house is wainscotted and has sliding window shutters. The building is furnished with family heirlooms. The earliest resident of the Follett house of whom we have record was Capt. Samuel Smallcorn, who had the fortune to have at various times occupied and owned the Piggin House, the Lady Pepperrell House, and Pepperrell Mansion. When Capt. Smallcorn died, his widow purchased of her two children their shares in their father's estate-houses, lands, wharves, and warehouses. When Robert Follett purchased the Piggin House of Jane Smallcorn, he was listed as a cooper of Kittery. Included in this purchase, in 1797, was a dwelling house, barn, warehouse, and wharf. No doubt, with these purchases, Follett turned from the cooper's profession to that of a merchant. Robert Follett married Mercy Mitchell, daughter of Joseph and Isabella Mitchell of **Mitchell Garrison**. They were the parents of five children John, Robert, Mary, Joshua Wentworth, and Mercy. Both John and Robert were merchants and sea captains. One of their ships took its name from the family connection, *The Two Brothers.* At the age of twenty-five Joshua Wentworth Follett sailed as first mate on a brig belonging to the Sheafes of Portsmouth. The vessel left Portsmouth Harbor in a severe gale, Nov. 15, 1797 but it broke up in the heavy seas and all hands were lost. Though four of these children were married, only one grandchild survived. Miss Mercy Follett, who for many years managed the family business, died in the Piggin House a spinster of seventy-two.

When Miss Mercy Follett died, in 1852, the Piggin House became the property of her nephew and sole heir Robert Follett Gerrish who was born on Gerrish Island. He inherited property and financial bequests from nearly all his grandparents. He brought the family fortune to its peak and lived to see it decline. He was a merchant engaged in trade with the West Indies. The last of Robert Follett Gerrish's children to live at the Piggin House was his daughter Caroline Lewis Gerrish,[113] who died in 1934. Miss Carrie Gerrish was a lady by birth and by training, a kind neigh-

---

113 Information on the Gerrish property was supplied by the late Miss Caroline Lewis Gerrish. Genealogical data comes from the parish burial ground.

bor, and a gracious friend to all who knew her. After her death, much of the enormous collection of family furniture was dispersed. The house became the property of her nephew Charles S. Gerrish of Portsmouth and Kittery Point.[114]

In 1840, at the height of the Gerrish-Follett fortune, Robert Follett Gerrish had the **William Pillow house**, next to the Piggin House, connected to it by a one hundred foot building which served as a dining room, while the Pillow house was a boarding house. In the center of the dining room was a well which remains though the dining room has long since been removed.

The **Gerrish warehouse** *(see Fig. 17)* is located near the Piggin House. This building, mentioned in Mrs. Smallcorn's sale of property, in 1797, is the only warehouse of its type left standing in Maine.[115] The Gerrish warehouse, when entered from the house is a one-story building; on the water-front side it is a two-story building. At the warehouse, foreign trade met domestic trade and made exchange of commodities. Domestic trade was transported in a vessel known as the gundalow, a craft adapted to river traffic. The gundalow was flat-bottomed and had a hinge in the mast so that the vessel could pass under bridges. At high tide it was anchored as close to the warehouse as possible. When the tide went out, the vessel was unloaded as it lay on the mud flats. The cargo was taken into the warehouse and lifted to the floor above by a huge wheel resembling a ferris wheel *(see Fig. 18)*. The old wharf, at which Follett and Gerrish ships docked, is gone, though traces of it remain. This wharf was the last of four wharves on Lawrence Cove, the Gerrish, Cutts, Sparhawk, and Cove Wharves. In 1909* a sign painted on the building read "Ship Stores and Medicines". The warehouse was evidently once a chandler store as well as being a storage place and a building for the exchange of foreign and domestic trade.

Before Robert Follett purchased the Piggin House, he owned a story and a half cottage that was built around 1767. This house is located at the end of Lawrence Lane and is the summer home of John N. M. Howells of New York. The house has been extensively remodeled but contains some early panelling, and other woodwork of interest. After Robert Follett purchased the Piggin House, this house became the home of his son Capt. John Follett. A pastel

---

114 Mr. Gerrish is a son of the late Follett Gerrish.
115 Another old warehouse is Sheafe's warehouse in Portsmouth, N. H. The Sheafe and Gerrish warehouses are among the few remaining examples of this type of building.
* Sylvester, *Old York*, p. 235

portrait of Robert Follett and an oil portrait of Capt. John Follett are owned by Charles S. Gerrish. The portraits show them to have been cultivated gentlemen of pleasing appearance. Robert Follett Sr. was captain of a company of Artillery at the fort at Kittery Point during the Revolution and became master of the Continental frigate *Raleigh.* Both John and Robert Jr. were captured aboard their ships during the War of 1812. John was confined a prisoner in Dartmoor and Robert, being lame and incapacitated, was put ashore in Maine by order of the English commander who made the capture. Capt. John Follett left no children and his widow became the first wife of Col. John Lawrence after whom Lawrence Lane was named. Col. Lawrence was childless by both marriages. (His second wife was a member of the Cutts family.) The Lawrences sold their cottage to Horace Mitchell Sr. who incorporated it as a part of the **Hotel Champernowne** property. From 1901 to 1926, the house remained a part of the hotel possessions, which changed hands three times. In 1926 the house was purchased by John Mead Howells of New York.

For several summers, in the late 1920s, the Hon. John Gilbert Winant of Concord, N. H., later U. S. Ambassador to Great Britain, was at the Point with his family. They leased the Robert Follett cottage and the Decatur cottage.

A little beyond the Howells estate on the shore is a house owned by Wyndham R. Mayo Jr. The house is small and quaint, very old in appearance. The building is one room wide pierced by a single chimney with large fireplaces. The building is at the water's edge. The panelling and some other woodwork are probably of a later date than the house, which, according to the records, would appear to have been built before 1674 by Roger Russell. It then became the property of **Capt. Francis Hooke**, a strong Gorges adherent, county treasurer of Yorkshire, judge, and kinsman of Humphrey Hooke, the lord mayor of Bristol who was influential in the founding of York, Maine. On the front of this house are piazzas placed there when the building housed the Portsmouth Yacht Club. The house belonged to Capt. Daniel Billings of Kittery who, in 1880, gave it to his grandson William G. Billings. Eight years later it was purchased by Mrs. Maria Decatur Mayo, daughter of Commodore Stephen Decatur, U. S. N., whose family had made Kittery their summer home for several years. Mrs. Mayo's daughter Maria (and her husband Rear Admiral

---

[116] Next to the Mayo house is an old Billings house, the summer residence of William Grace Billings, Jr. of Portsmouth, N. H. Howells, *Architectural Heritage of the Piscataqua*, p. 206, states that this house was built before 1794.

Morton Lindham Deyo, U.S. N.), together with the son Wyndham R. Mayo Jr. have been the owners of Francis Hooke's property through recent years. The building houses many pieces of furniture of the Decatur family who were descendants of the Gerrishes, Goodwins, Rices, Frosts and Pepperrells of Kittery.

A much beloved house in Kittery Point, the **1798 house** *(see Fig. 19)*, dressed in its warm red coating, surveys the harbor across a stretch of lawn and well-tended flower beds. This house, built by Capt. John Moore of Portsmouth,[117] was sold by him to Pelatiah Fernald, a sea captain. It is a one story house and stood across the street from one owned by Pelatiah Fernald's brother, the preacher Elder Mark Fernald.[118] The 1798 house remained in the hands of the Fernalds till 1897, when it was sold to George Savary Wasson,[119] artist and writer. The Wassons sold the house to Mrs. Elizabeth F. Paddock Upham of Portsmouth who lived here in some seclusion through the last years of her life. Since Mrs. Upham's death, in 1946, the 1798 house has been owned by her daughter Miss Frances Upham, a social worker. The interior of the 1798 house is of simple finish. It possesses two stairways and serves as a two-family dwelling.

The **1763 house** *(see Fig. 20)* resembles closely the 1798 house. It is occupied by tenants but is owned by Wilton P. Bray of Kittery Point who inherited it from his grandfather Isaac Deering Phillips. Mr. Bray and his cousin, Mrs. R. D. McDonough (formerly Marion Phillips) of Portsmouth say that, as far as they know, the house has always been in the possession of the Phillips family which would indicate that it was very likely built by Andrew Phillips, a soldier in the Revolutionary War.

On the north side of Pepperrell Road (at its intersection with Haley Road) is the residence of Merrill Pinkham, a one-story house which has changed hands many times. The earliest deed found mentioning this house is dated 1784. In that year, the house was sold by **James Kerswell**; Kerswell had kept an ordinary in the building *(see Fig. 21)*.

One of the most pleasing houses in Kittery Point is that which for convenience we may term the **1740 house**. This one story house, which

---

117 Moore's Island, lying directly before the 1798 house, takes its name from Capt. John Moore.
118 Elder Mark Fernald's autobiography tells much of Kittery life in the early nineteenth century, but concentrates on the elder's journeys in behalf of the Christian Church. Elder Fernald's house has been moved and now sits next to the Mitchell School. It is owned by Alden E. Finley.
119 For a biography of G. S. Wasson (Groveland, Mass., 1875 - Bangor, Maine, 1932), see *Who's Who in New England*, v. 1, p. 975. Wasson studied painting at the Royal Wurtenburg Art School. The house and studio he built at Kittery Point, in 1889, are owned by Miss Frances Upham. Two of the Liberty Ships of World War II were named after Kittery Point men, the *William Pepperrell* (sic), launched June 3, 1943, and the *George S. Wasson*, launched Dec. 7, 1943.

rambles about in every direction and culminates in a studio overlooking Chauncey's Creek and Gerrish Island, was purchased, in
1932, by Helen B. Knapp (Mrs. Farwell Knapp) of Hartford, Conn.,
niece of a well-known artist, the late Russel Cheney, who made his
home in Kittery. The Knapps have made extensive additions to the
house. Sheltered from the street by sumach and clinging to the bank
of Chauncey's Creek, the building is so well adapted to the terrain
that it seems more to have grown there than to have been built in
that place. Only the core of the house dates from 1740; [120] the larger
part of it was built by the Amee family who owned it for some time.
Evidence given by deeds would seem to indicate that the house was
the home of Capt. Samuel Mitchell, a shipwright of Kittery, who probably mentions it in his will in 1756.

It is unfortunate that a study cannot be made here of the buildings
that have been destroyed or that have survived only in part. I have mentioned earlier the **Andrew Pepperrell house** which stood on the same
location as the home of Charles Patey. This building, erected in 1747,
for Sir William's son whose love affair was blighted and who died at an
early age, was used to quarter troops during the Revolutionary War. The
troops chopped away the corner posts and the building was demolished
by a gale of wind.[121]   It was similar in appearance to Sparhawk Hall
which was built for Andrew Pepperrell's sister.

Pictures are extant of **Cutts House** on Cutts Island and **Gerrish
House** on Gerrish Island, both of which have been gone for many years.
The Cutts House (of which two drawings are owned by Joseph W. Cutts)
was a two-story house surrounded by trees and foliage. It was erected
in 1773 and demolished in 1880. This building stood on the site of
an earlier house erected by Capt. Francis Champernowne. Champernowne, a nephew of Sir Ferdinando Gorges, proprietor of Maine,
married the widow of Robert Cutts of Kittery. Champernowne owned
three houses, an upperhouse (on the site of the home of Charles Hart),
a lower house (where Miss Thaxter's residence stands today), and a
house in Greenland (named Greenland, the town taking its name
from his residence). For £200, Richard Cutts purchased, in 1742,
Champernowne's Island from his mother. His son Hon. Richard
Cutts, in 1773, erected on Cutts Island a house. He married a daughter of Joseph Curtis, innholder at Kittery and sheriff of York County.
Hon. Richard Cutts served as a major in Pepperrell's forces at Lou-

---

120 The date 1740 is cut into one of the beams of this house.
121 Safford, *Historic Homes of Kittery*. In *Collections of the Historical Society*, series 2, v. 5 (1895), p. 124.
122 Stackpole, *Old Kittery and Her Families*, p. 334.

isbourg in 1745. After his return he was a member of the Governor's council. Stackpole calls him one of the most eminent men of his time and place in Kittery, and says that he had a luxurious and hospitable residence on Cutts Island.[122] The Cutts Island property of Major Cutts passed to his son Judge Richard who married Sarah Frost of Frost Garrisons, Kittery (now Eliot), a great niece of Sir William Pepperrell and a granddaughter of Cutts' neighbors the Gerrishes. The eldest son of Judge Cutts, Capt. Joseph Cutts, lived at the Lady Pepperrell House. The second son Richard Cutts inherited the Cutts Island property and married Joanna Raynes who lived in the beautiful Raynes house in Seabury, York. The next owner of Cutts Island was William Wentworth Cutts, son-in-law of Richard. Oliver Cutts, administrator of W. W. Cutts' estate, sold the property, in 1880, to John and Roland Thaxter (sons of Celia Thaxter the poetess). The old house had been unpainted for the last fifty years of its history and needed extensive repairs. The Thaxters razed the building and on its site, incorporating many of the original timbers, erected a house which is standing, **Champernowne Farm** *(see Fig. 22)*, the residence of Miss Rosamond Thaxter and her mother, Mrs. Mary Gertrude Stoddard Thaxter. In 1880, the property, which had once been extensive, contained but one hundred thirty-seven acres. The same names Richard, John, Robert, Joseph, and Mary have persisted in the Cutts family over many generations. Joseph W. Cutts, the present Kittery Point representative of this family, has both a son and a nephew bearing the name of Richard Cutts. Mr. Cutts has a paper in his possession, which reads:

Anno Domini 1853

Cutts Island, Kittery, August 8th

The foundation of this chimney was laid August 6th. On Monday August 8th it was passed to the lower floor—today there are present – Lucy J. Cutts, Ellen H. Cutts, Mary Allen Gerrish, George H. Marden, Reuben Randall, Isaac Riley, Charles Abbott, and Richard Cutts. The latter is in his 89th year, is strong and vigorous but his reason is some impaired. Mr. Randall is the mason. The house is now occupied by William W. Cutts with his family, Mary J. and child Julia Emeline, five months old. William is at his store at Kittery Point, and his wife and child is on a visit at her father-in-law's at the same place Oliver Cutts – Eastman Cutts is now in New York and is mate of the ship Robert Parker. Formerly the house had but one chimney, and that in the middle. The old gentleman is quite enraged at the proposed plan of altering and having two chimneys, one at each end of the house. The prospects of good crops this season are favorable. Franklin Pierce is President of the Republic. The Worlds Fair is now in operation in New York. The business of the country is now in a prosperous condition – wages of day laborers are high – considerable excitement prevails in Europe – mostly between Austria Russia & Turkey. The Alms House is nearly completed being now ready for the painter.

Written by John H. Cutts
Per Order

This House is now 80 years old. The tree in front is 70.

Gerrish Island, the magnificent estate of the Hon. Timothy Gerrish, has but recently been sold by Gerrish descendants.[123] A small plot has been retained by some descendants, as well as the burial ground where the Hon. Timothy, his wife, and many descendants are buried. Timothy Gerrish was born in Dover, grandson of the redoubtable Indian fighter Maj. Richard Waldron who was finally tortured to death by the Indians. Timothy's wife, Sarah Eliot, daughter of Hon. Robert Eliot of New Castle and granddaughter of President Fryer of New Hampshire, received Gerrish Island as her wedding dowry. **Gerrish House** was probably built between 1706 and 1755. It was magnificently panelled, a house worthy of a great estate. A picture of the exterior of the building has been preserved in the sketch books of Miss Sarah Haven Foster, owned by the Portsmouth Public Library. The building, a two-story Georgian house, fronting the sea, stood on the site of the house known as the **Goodwin house**. The Gerrish home passed to Col Joseph Gerrish who was educated at Harvard and lived as a gentle man on his island estate. After the death of Col. Joseph Gerrish, in 1812, the Gerrish estate commenced to break up. Two of Col. Joseph's Gerrish grandsons were sea captains residing in Portsmouth. A third Gerrish grandson lived at the Follett house which his wife had inherited. The property passed from the Gerrish name but not from the Gerrish family. Col. Joseph's daughter, Anna, was mother of a large family including Gov. Ichabod Goodwin of New Hampshire and William H. Goodwin of Boston who bought up title to the Gerrish property. Gerrish House had passed beyond the state at which repair was possible, so it was torn down by William H. Goodwin who built another house on its site.

Ichabod Goodwin's grandson George Dewey (son of Admiral George Dewey) lived for some time in another old Gerrish house adjacent to the Goodwin estate. This property was the possession of Mrs. Greenough, a daughter of W. H. Goodwin; it is now owned by Capt. H. F. D. Davis, U. S. N. The house which has been much remodeled contains some excellent panelling.

---

123 Information regarding the Timothy Gerrish estate was gathered from Stackpole, *Old Kittery and Her Families*, and *The Island and Harbor Echo*, v. 3 no. 1 (Jan. 1896), and v. 4, no. 1, (Jan. 1897)

APPENDIX II

SOME OLD HOUSES IN KITTERY

WHIPPLE GARRISON, c. 1665. Whipple Garrison has beén considerably altered since its erection around 1665. The house is now fifty-four by thirty-four feet; Safford says it was once thirty-four feet square with an overhang, its timbers dovetailed at the comers. In 1859, extensive alterations of the house were made. Whipple Garrison is now 88 Whipple Road adjacent to Locke's Cove. In late colonial times, it was described as located at Whipple's Cove near Crooked Lane, for Crooked Lane was the name of the waterway lying between the present 88 Whipple Road and the U. S. Naval Base.

The date of Whipple Garrison is uncertain. Some writers have thought it was erected by the townspeople as a place of refuge; other writers (and this sounds more likely) have thought it was built by Capt. Robert Cutt after his return from Long Island. Robert was a brother of President John Cutt of New Hampshire. To this house Robert Cutt very likely brought his bride a gentlewoman from the Barbadoes. When Cutt died, his widow Mary became the wife of Capt. Francis Champernowne, nephew of the proprietor of Maine.

Whipple Garrison was the home next of Capt. Robert Cutt Jr., commander of one of Pepperrell's ships. Young Robert's sister Bridget had married the Rev. William Scriven a Baptist clergyman who built a house near the garrison. Scriven was the founder of the Baptist Church in Maine. Encountering persecution from the authorities Scriven left with a number of his wife's relatives and his flock; they became early settlers of Georgetown, South Carolina in which state many of their descendants have been prominent. Capt. Robert Cutt Jr. had no sons, only four daughters. One daughter married the Hon. John Moffatt who built the Moffatt Ladd house in Portsmouth, in 1762. Another daughter Mary became the wife of Capt. William Whipple, next owner of Whipple Garrison. The Whipples' eldest son, Gen. William Whipple, born in this house, achieved national reputation as a signer of the Declaration of Independence.

William Whipple was a sea captain engaged in the slave trade during his early life. He later became a business partner of his brother Col. Joseph Whipple, a Portsmouth merchant. As a member of the Continental Congress, as a representative to the New Hampshire Legislature, and as a justice of the New Hampshire Superior Court, Whipple (1730–1785) made a contribution to the new country. Whipple's wife was his cousin Catherine Moffatt at whose home he spent the last of his life.

Col. Joseph Whipple owned Whipple Garrison. He amassed a fortune in trade and land speculation (owning among other lots the entire township of Jefferson, N. H.). At Jefferson, N. H., he built a mansion, while at Portsmouth he owned a town house. Col. Joseph was Representative to the New Hampshire Legislature; he engaged in local politics and played the part of a typical country gentleman through the latter part of his life.

Col. Whipple's sister Mary married Robert Traill, Comptroller of the port of Portsmouth. Robert Traill had loyalist leanings and left Portsmouth at the outbreak of the Revolution. Since the colonel died childless, as did his brother the general, Whipple Garrison passed to the Traills' grandson Grame Keith Spence, a Baltimore merchant (Spence's sister was the mother of James Russell Lowell), who in turn sold it to a Portsmouth merchant Nathaniel Folsom. Folsom was a shipowner with extensive holdings in land. Through Hiram Keen and Alexander Nelson, the house passed, in 1839, to the Philbrick family who had recently come to Kittery from Rye, N. H. For ninety-eight years, members of the Philbrick family retained the house. The Philbricks and Wentworths placed their family tomb near the house. Lieut. Bryant A. Chandler, U. S. N., next owner of the house, sold it to Edwin D. Lee of Exeter, N. H., whose wife Rena B. Lee sold it to the present owners Mr. and Mrs. Francis L. Hatch. The Hatches have begun the restoration of the house. A memorial marker was placed on one wall of the house, in 1914, by the Daughters of the American Revolution.

FERNALD HOUSE, c. 1690 The Fernald house near Traip Academy is of simple construction but is very old. It has been little changed since it was built, it is said, about two hundred and sixty years ago. As the date of this building is not precise, I have given it the approximate date of 1690. Originally the house contained four rooms; an ell has been added in recent years. The pine board floors, large locks, fireplaces and Dutch oven, and the winding stairs are among the pleasing features of this house which faces Crooked Lane. Since 1931, the Fernald house has been owned by Mr. and Mrs. Henry S. Moore who have done much to preserve the building. During two years previous to the purchase by Mr. Moore, the house was the summer home of Philip Holmes, who acquired the building from the Fernald heirs. Miss Ann Louisa Fernald (1844-1928) lived here till her death. Miss Ann, known familiarly as "Aunt Ann" Fernald to a large circle of friends, was a daughter of Simon and Joanna (Williams) Fernald; she said that the building was an old Fernald house.

WILLOWBANK, c. 1727.Willowbank, according to some recent investigation, has probably been standing since 1727. Four rooms of the house comprise the original part of the building and even these rooms are much altered. The house was standing in 1735, at least, but it was a simple house then. Recent owners have made extensive changes. Willowbank is now an estate with landscaped grounds *(see Fig. 23)*, largely added by the Fendalls, Wendells, and Bensons. Former owners include the Brown, Cutts, and Austin families as well as those mentioned. The house has been, of late, the home of John P. Benson, marine painter, whose studio is located across Whipple Road from the house. Each year, Mr. Benson (who died in 1947) has had an exhibition of his paintings in the studio. A large proportion of Mr. Benson's work, painted since he moved to Kittery in 1925, is of local scenes. Willowbank is the birthplace of the present Countess of Carnarvon, formerly Lady Porchester, who was before marriage Ann Catherine Tredick Wendell, a descendant of an old Portsmouth family.

BADGER HOUSE, c. 1790. Only one wing of the Badger house *(see Fig. 24)* antedates the American Revolution. This wing which was sold by Aaron Witham, gentleman, and Elizabeth, his wife, to Samuel A. Badger, in 1819, is mentioned in deeds as early as 1790 when it belonged to the Witham family. The oldest part of this house has floorboards in the room above the kitchen, eighteen inches in width. Capt. Samuel Augustus Badger (1794-1857) was a nephew of the shipbuilders of Badger's Island, Robert and William Badger. Capt. Samuel built forty-five ships in Kittery. As his fortune increased, he increased his property holdings till they embraced a large part of what is now Kittery Foreside. The main part of the present Badger house, Capt. Samuel added, in 1824, while the west room was added at a still later date. Badger's bust is on his tombstone, at the rear of 16 Otis Avenue, once a part of Badger's estate. A number of portraits of the Badgers hang in the hallway of this house. The building is located at the water's edge, facing Badger's Island. One of Badger's three sons, Capt. George W. Badger, became master of his own vessel at the age of twenty-two. He was master of the brig *Apphia Maria* of New Orleans when he contracted yellow fever and died in that city at the age of twenty-two. Another son, Samuel Augustus Badger, after graduating from Yale, became a member of the New Hampshire Legislature and drew up the papers for the incorporation of the city of Portsmouth, in 1849. The house at Kittery became the residence of Capt. Samuel's daughter Mrs. John Neal (Ann M. Badger) and is today the summer home of her granddaughters the Misses Alison, Annie, and Carrie Locke of Jacksonville, Florida. The last full-rigged ship to be launched from Samuel's shipyard was the *Granite State*, built in 1877 by John Neal.[124]

RICE HOUSE, c. 1750. A story and a half house, on the corner of Government Street and Rice Avenue, sits with its surrounding land in lone dignity on a rise overlooking the Piscataqua and Badger's Island. The house has been closed for several years and the grounds have not received care. The property, though much curtailed, possesses a surprising amount of land in an area which has been built up with small homes. The house of Samuel Rice has a fair amount of old woodwork though the exterior has been altered. Samuel Rice was half-owner of the ferry from Kittery to Portsmouth. When he died, in 1791, his estate was divided among a large number of children who achieved considerable prominence in this section of New England. One son, Alexander, was a bridge builder and tavern keeper. Among the bridges he built was one crossing the York River which, though it has been rebuilt many times, yet bears the name of Rice's Bridge. Rice Tavern, a beautifully panelled house (demolished around 1940), was located near the old house. Photographs of the tavern are owned by Miss Dorothy M. Vaughan of Portsmouth. The last member of the Rice family to live at the Tavern was Miss Sarah Ann Elizabeth Rice, a devout communicant of St. John's Church in Portsmouth and a belle dame of her time; Miss Rice died in 1874. Sarah Orne Jewett has described in one of her published letters a visit to the old tavern where her relative lived. Miss Jewett's grandfather and her uncle had both married members of the Rice family.

One of Samuel Rice's granddaughters was married to Governor Ichabod Goodwin of New Hampshire, and a great-granddaughter to Admiral George Dewey, U. S. N. Samuel's eldest son, John, served in the militia during the Revolutionary War, while another son, Samuel Jr., commanded the privateer ships *Fancy, Retaliation,* and *Satisfaction.* Capt. Samuel Rice Jr. was captured by the British, in 1778, and imprisoned in Dartmoor Prison in England. He was grandfather of Miss Arabella Rice of Portsmouth who died in 1872, leaving many philanthropic bequests, among them

---

[124] The *Granite State*, 1684 tons, owned by Daniel Marcy of Portsmouth, was the largest ship to be built here. She was lost in 1898, on the Needles, off the Lizard in Cornwall. Information on the *Granite State* (the second ship by that name) was supplied by William E. Dennett of Kittery, Maine.

a donation of $30,000, in memory of her father, Robert Rice, establishingthe Rice Free Public Library of Kittery. Another son of old Samuel was Capt. William Rice of Portsmouth, who, like his brother, made a fortune from privateering. In 1814, a party was held at his Portsmouth house. Relatives and friends were invited to cut from the bales of calico, captured by his privateers from English ships, all the dress patterns they could carry home. One of William Rice's sisters married Capt. William Dennett Jr.; they owned the island, then called Dennett's Island, on which the U. S. Naval Base was erected, and built the house (moved and remodeled in 1818) which is the residence of the commandant of the Naval Base at Portsmouth. Two other sisters of William were the successive wives of William Badger (1752-1830) of Badger's Island. Badger had moved to Kittery from Newfields, N. H. He became the outstanding ship builder of his time in this vicinity, and erected a mansion on Badger's Island near his shipyard. Badger built nearly a hundred ships naming the last one after himself.

The old Rice house became the property of the Langton family. Mr. John Langton and his blind daughter Miss Hattie Langton lived together for many years. After the father's death, Miss Langton moved to Brooklyn, New York, where she met a tragic death. Most of the time since the Langtons left it, the old Rice house has been closed.

DENNETT HOUSE, c. 1710. The driveway leading to the Dennett house *(see Fig. 25)* from Dennett Road is lined with elms and locusts. The sharp, high roof and single massive chimney of this house give it a venerable appearance. It was erected, in 1710, by John Dennett of Portsmouth, but is not the oldest Dennett house now standing. A Dennett house (owned by Joseph St. Pierre), much altered, is located on Christian Shore in Portsmouth, at the head of Dennett Street; this house, built in 1680, was long known as "The Beehive". The Dennetts have usually been active in local government.

John Dennett Sr. and his son Ephraim Dennett were for many years selectmen of Portsmouth. John Dennett Jr. and his son William were for many years selectmen of Kittery, while William's son Mark and grandson Alexander Dennett were members of both houses of the state legislature of Maine. William E. Dennett is at present one of the selectmen of Kittery.

Major Mark Dennett at the age of eighteen commenced to teach school in Kittery; he continued to do so, save for two or three years, until he reached the age of sixty. He did much to raise the position of education in Kittery; in recognition of this service the town named the Wentworth-Dennett School after him. Major Mark Dennett's papers have been of much assistance to all of Kittery's historians. Major Dennett died in 1883; his descendants by the names of Dennett, Marshall, Burnham, and Withington have continued the traditions of service established by the early Dennetts.

The house has remained in the family for nearly two hundred and fifty years. It is owned by Lieutenant Commander Ralph Dennett, U. S. N., whose branch of the family has provided the country with many officers in the Navy and Coast Guard service. The present owner of the old house has restored the building, so that while historic features have been preserved it has become a comfortable home *(see Fig. 26)*. It is one of the most interesting houses architecturally to be found in Kittery. The present chimney is massive but not as large as the original which was built in a shape similar to the quadrate cross, like the chimney of the Jabez Fitch house in Portsmouth. The building is thirty by forty feet with large fireplaces. The lower story walls are constructed of hewn hemlock dovetailed and treenailed together, while the upper story is of oak. The staircase is Jacobean in style with oak rail and spindles, the latter showing heavily turned work, said to have come from the Dennett house at Christian Shore. Two landings take one to the second story; a small door on the second landing opens to a passageway completely encircling the chimney. The hall chamber is panelled, like the room below, with fluted columns on either side of a finely proportioned fireplace. The house was listed, in 1720, as a place of refuge from Indian depredations.

SHAPLEIGH HOUSE, c. 1735. Between 1730 and 1740, Capt. John Shapleigh, great-grandson of Kittery Point's first settler and proprietor, built a house which is standing, though in dilapidated condition, across the road from the Shapleigh School in North Kittery. Capt. Shapleigh's father had been killed by the Indians. From his mother he inherited a large tract of land which had been owned by her father Thomas Withers, a supporter of Gorges and an extensive landholder in early Kittery. Wither's land was divided among his three daughters—Mrs. Rice, Mrs. Curtis, and Mrs. Shapleigh.

Capt. John Shapleigh was a well-to-do farmer and captain of the local militia. The house has descended through Capt. John Nicholas, Dennis F. and Charles F. Shapleigh to Dr. Edward Everett Shapleigh of Kittery, the present owner.

The last occupant of the house, Charles F. Shapleigh, died in 1906. For many years, the property was held by a large number of heirs, so it was neglected. The result was disastrous for eventually the house had to be abandoned. It is a picturesque ruin with its large chimney and gray weathered walls, standing amidst the lilac bushes. Unfortunately, it is a ruin that cannot be long with us; a photograph of the house is owned by Douglas Armsden of Kittery *(see Fig. 27)*.

DODOVAH CURTIS HOUSE, bef. 1700. When Thomas Withers divided his land, he willed to his daughter Elizabeth a large tract of land in North Kittery. Despite this sizeable inheritance, poor Elizabeth had an unhappy life. She was left a widow with two sons at an early age; both sons died before marriage. The youngest son, Withers Berry, had been elected a representative to the General Court at Boston; he was accidentally thrown from the ferry while crossing the Charles River in December. Berry remained so long in the icy water that he died from exposure. Elizabeth's second husband, Dodovah Curtis is reputed to have built this house. The only child by the second marriage was killed by the Indians in 1705.

John Shapleigh (father-in-law of Gen. Fernald of Eliot), in 1762, sold the house to Capt. Richard Keating of Kittery, a sea captain, who kept an inn here. When Richard died, the house became the property of his son Richard Jr. who had married Sally Sayward Barrell of Barrell Grove. Mrs. Keating (1759-1855), later Madam Wood, was one of America's early novelists—one of the first women in America whose writings were printed. She commenced publishing shortly after leaving this house and may have done some of her writing here. The titles of her works we find amusing, as *Julia and the Illuminated Baron* and *Amelia or the Influence of Virtue*. A few months before he died, in 1783, Richard Keating sold the house to Edward Sargent. From Sargent the house passed to Thomas Hutchings Lewis and his son Enoch Hutchings Lewis.

The Lewises and Haleys intermarried and numerous real estate transactions passed between them. In 1856, the house passed from Thomas Haley to his son-in-law Henry B. Manson; the next year it was divided into two parts. One part is now incorporated into the residence of Mrs. Elmer Lewis on Haley Road. The other part was moved to its present location on Spruce Creek, from the old location across the present Maine Turnpike *(see Fig. 28)*. It required twenty-two yoke of oxen to haul the building. Manson had intended to place the house farther from the road but moving tackle broke and the house remained, close to what is now

U.S. Highway No. 1, formerly the Post Road.

Though it changed hands a few times, the house has returned to the family of Thomas Haley; from Thomas Jackson Pettegrew it passed to his daughter the present owner Pearle Edna Pettegrew Chick (Mrs. Willard C. Chick). Other outstanding women than Mrs. Keating have made this their home at times. Long visits have been made here by Mrs. Chick's sisters Dr. Augusta Pettegrew Shute, a physician, who was Treasurer-General of the Daughters of the American Revolution in Washington, D. C., and Miss Susan Evelyn Pettegrew (Kittery, 1866–Boston, 1919). After graduating from Gorham Normal School, in 1885, Susan Evelyn became "Sister Evelyn Margaret" at the Episcopal convent on Louisburg Square in Boston, in 1900. She was the fiftieth sister to enter the Order of St. Margaret. Sister Evelyn Margaret did much mission work among the colored people of Philadelphia.

The Curtis house has three interesting rooms, the West room, the chamber above it, and the hall. The stairway, set against the chimney, is steep and looks as though built at an early date. The lower West room has window seats and some fine panelling and cornices.

THE DR. DANIEL PIERCE HOUSE, 1763. At the head of Spruce Creek, in 1763, Dr. Daniel Pierce of Newbury (Mass.) built his home. The doctor did not appreciate the magnificent view of the creek, for he built his house facing the road. The present owners, Dr. and Mrs. E. Petrie Hoyle, who have owned the house since 1930, purchased the place because of the location. From the drawing room one has a full view of the creek and of the landscaped grounds sloping to the water. The building possesses no woodwork of outstanding quality, but the view from the house makes this place well worth mentioning. The house has been arranged so that the view is emphasized.

In the cellar may be seen a massive chimney in which is cut the inscription: "James Fernald, 1763." Very likely Fernald was the mason who constructed this chimney.

Dr. Daniel Pierce had his office in his home, and a miniature drug store as well as a post-office. Dr. Pierce was the sole physician in Kittery during a large part of his life. Very few of Dr. Pierce's nine children remained in Kittery. One son Charles became a printer and publisher, at first in Portsmouth and later in Philadelphia. Many of the early Portsmouth imprints are from the printing press of Charles Pierce. Three Daniel Pierces, in succession, owned this house. The third Daniel Pierce was the grandfather of Dr. George Loring Pierce and Dr. Edward Everett

Shapleigh, both of Kittery. Dr. G. L. Pierce lived in this house, and his daughter-in-law (the widow of Dr. Daniel J. Pierce) sold the house to Dr. E. Petrie Hoyle. This house has, in one way or another, been associated with the medical profession throughout most of its history.

ADDITIONAL DATA

While this work was in the press, further information on the Billings house (page 69, footnote 116) was found. This building was the home of Lieut. Daniel Billings, who fought in the Revolutionary War, and later of his son Ephraim. Ephraim's three sons, Robert, Daniel, and Samuel (all sea captains) and his daughter Eliza, were born in this house. Eliza lived here till she died a spinster of sixty-seven years. Capt. Samuel commanded a great many ships, among them the Kittery-built *Granite State*. In a Kittery-built bark, the *Apphia Maria*, he transported troops to Mexico during the Mexican War. Samuel Billings' ship was the first American vessel to sail up the river Seine to Rouen; it carried a cargo of cotton from New Orleans. This picturesque house is noticeable at once, because of its Beverly Ears, which give it second story windows looking seaward. How often from these windows the Billings must have scanned the horizon as the captains sailed away and came back again to port!

APPENDIX III
Prepared by Thomas Prince

Colonial Village was written by John Eldridge Frost in 1947 to document the history of homes and other structures built in Kittery prior to 1800. These structures are referred to as "colonial." The updates that follow were compiled in February 2021 to record the current status and what transpired with these structures over the 74 years since *Colonial Village* was first published.

The appendix is sorted by the following homes/structures as listed in the book's table of contents.

Main Section
Bray House, Lady Pepperrell House, Pepperrell Mansion (William Pepperrell House), Sparhawk Hall, Mitchell Garrison, Fort McClary, Joan Deering House, Congregational Church Parsonage, First Parish Church

Appendix I (other homes/structures in Kittery Point)
Major Cutts' Store, Pepperrell Counting House, The Piggin House, Gerrish Warehouse, Robert Follett House, The Hooke House, 1798 House, 1763 House, The Kerswell Ordinary, 1740 House, Cutts House, Gerrish House
Appendix II (other homes/structures in Kittery)
Whipple Garrison, Willowbank, Fernald House, Badger House, Rice House, Dennett House, Shapleigh House, Dodovah Curtis House, Dr. Daniel Pierce House

BRAY HOUSE
See Main Section, Page 9. (*Figure 1*)
Date built: 1662 (1720)
Street Address: 100 Pepperrell Road, Kittery Point

Summary prior to 1947 as noted in Colonial Village *and other sources:*

An original house is estimated built in 1662 by John Bray, shipwright. The Bray House is widely considered one of the oldest houses in Maine. It faces Pepperrell Cove.

After 1947 and current status:

- The structure was added to the National Register of Historic Places in 1979.

- The Bray House has stayed as the original structure for its lifetime. Over the years, several additions were made to the property. One of those added structures was the Hoyt House, built in 1850.

- In 2007 Daryl Hall of the rock duo Hall & Oates bought the home and adjoining structures. He undertook a partial restoration including extensive interior upgrades. He then sold the house in 2014.

- The new owners drew up plans for major changes to the Bray House property. Their plans called for demolition of all buildings and structures on the property, except for the Bray House. The plans called for modernizing the surrounding structures while showcasing the original Bray home. The plans were met with some local opposition; however the plans were presented to the Kittery Planning Board in 2015 and approved.

- Today, the original Bray House still stands and is the centerpiece of the property. It is the only two-story building on the property. It is now flanked with several modern, one story, angular shaped buildings.

- According to recent estimates, the year built for the present house is recorded as 1720. There is mention of an original house built in 1662, which may be incorporated into the 1720 structure.

LADY PEPPERRELL HOUSE

See Main Section, Page 14. (*Figures 2, 3, 4*)
Date built: 1760
Street Address: 24 Pepperrell Road, Kittery Point

Summary prior to 1947 as noted in Colonial Village *and other sources:*

This high-Georgian style house sits on a sharp corner of Pepperrell Road opposite the Congregational Church. It was built in 1760 for the widow of Sir William Pepperrell shortly after his death in 1759.

After 1947 and current status:

- In 1942 the house was given to the Society for Preservation of New England Antiquities, now Historic New England. The interior of the building experienced a major fire in December, 1945. Following, it was meticulously restored and maintained. Additionally, the deteriorated porch was fully reconstructed to its original condition.

- The house was designated a National Historic Landmark in 1960. It was listed on the National Register of Historic Places in 1966.

- In 1985 Historic New England sold the home into private hands while retaining preservation and conservation easements to limit alterations. Today it remains a private home but is open to the public occasionally.

PEPPERRELL MANSION (WILLIAM PEPPERRELL HOUSE)

See Main Section, Page 22. (*Figures 5, 6)*
Date built: 1682
Street Address: 94 Pepperrell Road, Kittery Point

Summary prior to 1947 as noted in Colonial Village *and other sources:*

The house was built in 1682 by Col. William Pepperrell on land deeded to him by his father-in-law, John Bray. It was located next door to the Bray House. The home was the birthplace and home of Sir William Pepperrell, Col. William Pepperrell's son, who was knighted by King George II of Britain for his leadership and financial assistance in the successful capture of Louisbourg on Cape Breton Island, Canada from the French in 1745. Many famous folks have toured or visited the Pepperrell Mansion including Nathaniel Hawthorne, who wrote about his tour of the house in 1847. The home was later that of John Haley Bellamy, noted carver of the Bellamy eagles and figureheads. It is called the Pepperrell Mansion because of the magnificent interior woodworking.

After 1947 and current status:

• The home is currently standing in its original location and is well maintained.

• The home was entered in the National Register of Historic Places in 1973.

• The home was in the possession of the Frost family from the mid-1940s until 1978. The last Frost owners were Joseph and John Frost. In 1978 it was purchased by Booth and Mary Hemingway. The Hemingways sold the house in 1996.

• Joe Frost often repurposed finds from other buildings. The parapets over the windows and door on the water side and west side of the house were repurposed from the Sparhawk Mansion when it was demolished in 1967. A kitchen and garage were added around 1978. In 2001 the 1978 addition had an upper floor added for a family room. In the 1990s a new kitchen was put in, as was a master bath remodel. Colonial features were preserved.

• The current owner refurbished the entire house, paying close attention to managing and repairing the exceptional woodwork that was added to the house during the 1723 remodel.

SPARHAWK HALL

See Main Section, Page 27. (*Figures 8 and 9*)
Date built: 1742
Street Address: off Sparhawk Lane in an area behind the Congregational Church, Kittery Point

Summary prior to 1947 as noted in Colonial Village *and other sources:*

This elaborate wooden house was built by Sir William Pepperrell for his daughter Elizabeth upon her marriage in 1742 to Nathaniel Sparhawk. It was crowned with an elegant cupola. The house contained finely carved paneling in 19 rooms.

After 1947 and current status:

- The home no longer exists.

- In 1949 the house had a role in Louis de Rochemont's 1949 movie, "Lost Boundaries," serving as the fictional home of Dr. Scott Carter.

- By the early 1950s Horace Mitchell, Jr., and his family were living in only four rooms in the house, having closed off the other rooms. (Horace Mitchell, Sr. had bought the home in 1902). The house was very expensive to heat and maintain so the Mitchells decided to sell approximately 75% of the home to Norman Woolworth of New York and Winthrop, Maine. Woolworth was a member of the wealthy Woolworth family. This included the large drawing room hall, original stairway, dining room, the southwest bedroom, and a small room near the rear hall.

- In January 1953 the paneling, floors, and other parts of the rooms were dismantled and shipped to Winthrop, Maine where they were used in another building. In March 1953 the Mitchell family moved out of Sparhawk Hall and into a nearby home they had recently constructed.

- The empty Sparhawk Hall was subsequently acquired in 1965 by Strawbery Banke, Inc. of Portsmouth through the generosity of Miss Rosamond Thaxter, with the hope it could be saved and perhaps moved to Portsmouth. However, because of the home's much deteriorated condition, salvage was not possible. Thereafter, Strawbery Banke, Inc. removed all remaining fixtures and features worth salvaging. This included the front door and casing, which were sent to the Boston Museum of Fine Arts, where they are currently on display.

- In 1967 the house was razed and burned with the assistance of the Kittery Fire Department. The remaining refuse was hauled to the Kittery town dump.

- Today, there is another home located on the site where Sparhawk Hall once stood. This home was moved from another location in town and is reported to sit on the Sparhawk Hall foundation.

MITCHELL GARRISON

See Main Section, Page 34. (*Figure 10*)
Date built: c. 1700
Street Address: off Brave Boat Harbor Road, Kittery Point

Summary prior to 1947 as noted in Colonial Village and other sources:

- The Mitchell Garrison, now commonly referred to as the Andrews-Mitchell Garrison, stood on high ground near the York line, with a commanding view of Brave Boat Harbor. First built as a one-room dwelling with a fireplace, it soon was expanded to accommodate a second family. The house nearly doubled in size to two rooms, and another fireplace was added. Although small, it was designated as a "garrison" for other neighboring families, a fortified structure that might offer these early settlers protection when dealing with Indian raids, which started in 1675 and lasted nearly a century.

After 1947 and current status:

- The house no longer sits on its original site.

- In the late 1970s, Capt. Sidney and Beatrice Helliwell gave the Garrison to the Kittery Historical and Naval Museum with the hope that it would one day serve as a learning tool for generations to come. After the modern additions were stripped away, the Museum had the timbers of the original structure, dating back at least to the early 1700s, carefully numbered, dismantled, and stored.

- After a successful fund-raising drive in 2002 and groundbreaking in October 2003, the Museum constructed an addition in the rear of the Museum building on Rogers Road. They then took on the ambitious project of reassembling one section of the Garrison. Dedication of the addition and exhibit was held in October 2006. Visitors to the Museum were then able to walk around the exterior of the Garrison, viewing the actual timbers of the original home. Visitors could also view the home's interior features supported by period-attired mannequins posed as if going through a day's routine. The featured furniture and items are period correct (1722). Displays of photos and narratives were added to the exhibit to inform Museum visitors of the historical nature of the preserved home.

FORT McCLARY

See Main Section, Page 39. (*Figure 11*)
Date built: 1715
Street Address: 46 Pepperrell Road, Kittery Point

Summary prior to 1947 as noted in Colonial Village *and other sources:*

Since 1715 a fort has stood at this location to protect the approaches to the Piscataqua River. First called Fort William, the name was changed to Fort McClary in 1808, named after Major Andrew McClary, who died in the Revolutionary War. The present buildings represent several different periods of construction. The site was manned during five wars; however, like most Maine forts, it saw little conflict. The distinctive blockhouse dates from 1844. By the 1910s the fort had fallen into disrepair and it was officially decommissioned in 1918. The State of Maine acquired most of the property from the federal government in 1924, after which it was managed as a park.

After 1947 and current status:

• Fort McClary was entered in the National Register of Historic Places in 1969.

• The blockhouse and other structures were renovated in 1987. The blockhouse now serves as a museum.

• Today, the property and its surviving structures continue to be owned and operated by the State of Maine as the Fort McClary State Historic Site. It continues to be a very popular site for people who live in or travel to the Southern Maine area.

JOAN DEERING HOUSE

See Main Section, Page 45. (*Figure 12*)
Date built: 1700
Street Address: 111 Pepperrell Rd., Kittery Point

Summary prior to 1947 as noted in Colonial Village *and other sources:*

Joan Deering, born in 1662, was the daughter of John Bray (see the Bray House). She was the younger sister of Margery Mary Pepperrell, whose husband was Col. William Pepperrell (see the Pepperrell Mansion). Joan was married to Clement Deering. He passed away around 1695. This house was built as a tavern and dwelling for Joan Deering in 1700. She lived in the home and operated it as tavern for only a few years, as she passed away in 1708.

After 1947 and current status:

- The home still stands in its original location. It has remained as a private residence for most of its lifetime.

- No significant changes or modifications have been made over the last 74 years except for the ongoing maintenance projects required to preserve the home and keep it in good shape.

- Other than the woodwork around the fireplace, many of the original colonial features of the home have either been replaced or upgraded over the past centuries by the owners. There is no evidence of its past use as a tavern.

- The property in the rear of the home consists of nearly three acres of undeveloped land that was included in the original tract of land when the home was built 300 years ago. Today's property also includes a carriage house and a barn.

CONGREGATIONAL CHURCH PARSONAGE

See Main Section, Page 50. (*Figure 13)*
Date built: 1729
Street Address: 23 Pepperrell Road, Kittery Point

Summary prior to 1947 as noted in Colonial Village *and other sources:*

The old parsonage for the First Congregational Church was built in 1729 for the first pastor, Rev. John Newmarch, who served at the church for more than 50 years. A new parsonage was built in 1910. Since 1910 the old parsonage has served as a parish and community hall. In 1938 a one-and-a-half-story gable-roofed ell was attached to the rear of the building.

After 1947 and current status:

- After World War II with the resulting increase in Kittery's population, the old parsonage wasn't big enough to support Sunday School or other church activities. As a result, in 1958 an annex was added to the building, providing more room in the large hall and another Sunday school room upstairs. Additionally, a parking lot was built and paved.

- The old parsonage was entered into the National Register of Historic Places in 1978, at the same time the church was entered (see the next entry).

- A half-million-dollar renovation to the old parsonage/parish hall was completed in 2005. The new addition included a commercial style kitchen, new bathrooms, three storage rooms, and a new stairway and exit from the full second story, where the area of the original kitchen attic became a meeting room. A classroom used as the nursery, a storage room for the Women's Fellowship, and a second larger meeting room were also added.

FIRST PARISH CHURCH (FIRST CONGREGATIONAL CHURCH)

See Main Section, Page 56. (*Figures 2, 14, 15*)
Date built: 1730
Street Address: 23 Pepperrell Road, Kittery Point

Summary prior to 1947 as noted in Colonial Village *and other sources:*

The First Parish Church, now known as The First Congregational Church, is a historic church located across the street from the Lady Pepperrell House. The church was organized in 1714 where members first gathered in a meeting house. The church building was built in 1730 and completed in 1732. It is the oldest church building in Kittery, and one of the oldest in the state of Maine. Several alterations have been done over the years. In 1840 it was remodeled with Greek revival details. In 1874 the church building was moved back from what is now the middle of the road. This was done at the request of the town so the road could be improved. In 1892, the belfry was capped with a segmental dome.

Associated with the church and located directly across Pepperrell Road is an old burying ground. This cemetery is about 1 acre and believed to date to 1733. It is surrounded on three sides by a low stone wall, and on the fourth by the Piscataqua River. Burials in the cemetery date from the mid-18th century into the 21st century.

After 1947 and current status:

- To the present day, the church and old parsonage/parish hall continue to provide religious and community activities for citizens of Kittery Point and the surrounding area.
- The church building and original parsonage were entered into the National Register of Historic Places in 1978.
- The old burial ground was entered into the National Register of Historic Places in 1997. While the burial ground was mentioned in the

church's entry in the Register in 1978, it was not fully documented. Thus, to update the Register, an additional entry for a "boundary increase" and detailed description of the cemetery were added in 1997.

- In the early 21st century the dome was re-coppered, a memorial garden was created, and a rebuilding of the cemetery wall was completed.

MAJOR CUTTS' STORE

See Appendix I, page 66. (*Figure 16*)
Date built: c. 1790
Street Address: 88 Pepperrell Road, Kittery Point

Summary prior to 1947 as noted in Colonial Village *and other sources:*

Major Thomas Cutts, who lived at the Pepperrell Mansion, kept a store next to his home. In 1828, the Frisbees purchased the store and in that year Daniel Frisbee doubled the size of the old Cutts' Store resulting in a high pitch roof line. The Frisbees operated it as a store until 1908 when they opened a new market in a building they constructed closer to Pepperrell Road. After opening the new market, the old Cutts' store became a sort of ship chandlery (boat paint, hardware, rope, etc.)

After 1947 and current status:

- A small restaurant was added alongside the ship chandlery in the late 1960s called Cap'n Simeon's Sandwich Shop. It had an area inside with a few tables for the patrons. The ship chandlery closed down soon after, and the restaurant was expanded and renamed Cap'n Simeon's Galley which operated until 2010. The beams in the front of the restaurant were all that were left of the original Cutts' Store.

- Following a major fire in June 2016 at Frisbee's Market, all the property was sold to new owners, including the original Cutts' Store building, which was then a restaurant, and the Frisbee's Market building.

- The site of the former Cap'n Simeon's Galley was expanded and refurbished and is now a function space called The View. The first floor of the Frisbee's Market building was made into a restaurant called Bistro 1828 and the third floor is a bar with outdoor roof deck called The Ski Club (commemorating the Pepperrell Cove Water Ski Club from the 1950s). These businesses opened in 2019.

PEPPERRELL COUNTING HOUSE

See Appendix I, Page 66. *(Figure 7)*
Date built: 1710
Street Address: 94 Pepperrell Road, Kittery Point

Summary prior to 1947 as noted in Colonial Village *and other sources:*

This building was originally under ownership of the Pepperrells and used in their merchant and trade business. It was located between the Pepperrell Mansion and the Pepperrell wharves. In later years the old timbers in the building were remodeled by wood carver John Haley Bellamy and the building was used as his carving shop. In more recent times it was adapted as a studio cottage. Winslow Homer and Mark Twain were visitors with Bellamy in the late 19th century,

After 1947 and current status:

• The building still stands today in its original location adjacent to the Town of Kittery wharf and boat landing. The house has remained a part of the Pepperrell Mansion property over the years. During the ownership of Joe Frost, he repurposed the brick walkway leading to the counting house from bricks taken from an 18th century church in Portsmouth.

• The counting house was primarily a rental property of past owners. Under the current ownership, it now serves as a guest house. It has been refurbished and retains many of the details from the time it was John Haley Bellamy's workshop.

THE "PIGGIN HOUSE" (A.K.A. ROBERT F. GERRISH HOUSE)

See Appendix I, Page 66. *(Figure 17)*
Date built: 1700
Street Address: 6 Follett Lane, Kittery Point

Summary prior to 1947 as noted in Colonial Village *and other sources:*

The original part of the house was built in 1700 and was known as the "Piggin House." In the late 1700s it was acquired by Capt. Samuel Smallcorn who sold it in 1797 to Robert Follett, Jr. At the time it was a two-story house with the chimney at one end. Following Robert's death, the home came into the possession of his sister Mary who married William Thompson Gerrish in 1814. They doubled the size of the structure to the west end, thus bringing the chimney into the middle of the home. William and Mary Gerrish had a son named Robert Follett Gerrish who gained ownership of the home after his parents' death in the mid-1800s. Thereafter the home was called the Robert F. Gerrish House. When *Colonial Village* was published in 1947 the home was owned by Charles Gerrish, Sr., a descendent of Robert F. Gerrish. The property also housed the Gerrish Warehouse on the river's edge, and a barn.

After 1947 and current status:

- The home still stands in its original location. It is well maintained. It continues to remain in the Gerrish family as a private residence. The barn and warehouse no longer exist (see below: 'Gerrish Warehouse'). After Charles Gerrish, Sr. died in 1975, ownership of the home was passed to his daughter, Marian Gerrish Craig. She and her husband, Robert Craig, maintained the home for themselves and family until Mrs. Craig's death in 2015.

- As noted in Colonial Village on page 68, on the same property and next door to the "Piggin House" was another home owned by Robert Gerrish called the William Pillow House. The "Pillow House" was in a much-deteriorated condition by the early 1990s, when it was demolished. A new home was constructed in its location in 1994 and is now the residence of Donald Craig, son of Marian Gerrish Craig. Also on the property was a small seasonal cabin, called "Ditty Box," which was popular in the early part of the 20th century and was rented during the summer months to artists and other clientele. It burned to the ground in 1969.

THE GERRISH WAREHOUSE

See Appendix I, page 68. (*Figures 17 and 18)*
Date built: 1710
Street Address: 6 Follett Lane, Kittery Point

Summary prior to 1947 as noted in Colonial Village *and other sources:*

The warehouse, built c. 1710, was once a part of the large shipping empire of the Pepperrell family. The building was part of William Pepperrell's estate until after the Revolutionary War when the State of Massachusetts confiscated it due to the Pepperrells' empathy with the British. Samuel Smallcorn bought it at auction from the state in 1778 and sold it in 1797 to Robert Follett, Jr. Follett owned it until his death, and thereafter his sister Mary gained ownership following her marriage to William Thompson Gerrish. The Gerrish family used the building, now called the Gerrish Warehouse, as a store and ship chandlery for many years. William and Mary Gerrish had a son named Robert Follett Gerrish, who acquired ownership in the mid-1800s after the death of his parents. He used the warehouse as a store, post office, and notary public's office until his death in 1882; thereafter, the warehouse was no longer used for commercial purposes.

After 1947 and current status:

- Marian Gerrish Craig and her brother, Charles Gerrish, Jr., sold the warehouse to the Maine Maritime Museum of Bath, Maine in 1976. The museum developed plans to move the building to a more secure location, as its foundation was being undermined by tidal erosion.

- The building was added to the National Register of Historic Places in 1977.

- Subsequently, the Maritime Museum attempted to move the building; however, the plans were not realized as the building was considered too far decayed. The Museum removed the contents and salvaged what could be saved and then the building was demolished. The contents remain in storage at the Museum in Bath.

- The warehouse was removed from the Register of Historic Places in September 2015.

ROBERT FOLLETT HOUSE

See Appendix I, Page 67.
Date built: 1765
Street Address: 11 Lawrence Lane, Kittery Point

Summary prior to 1947 as noted in Colonial Village *and other sources:*

This house was originally built around 1767 and was the home of Robert Follett, Sr. Following his death in 1780, the home became the property of his son John. In 1890 Horace Mitchell, Sr. bought the house and adjacent property, where he erected the Hotel Champernowne. Following Mitchell's death, John Mead Howells purchased both the home and hotel. In 1926 Howells razed the hotel while keeping the Robert Follett House. He upgraded the house for the use of his son William White Howells. The upgrade included a beautiful and distinctive front door and covered entrance that John Mead Howells repurposed from an old home in Portsmouth, NH in 1930.

After 1947 and current status:

- A major upgrade and significant makeover of the Robert Follett House was undertaken over an 18-month period from 2006-2008. At the beginning of the construction, the Howells wanted to save certain historic features of the Follett House. One historic feature that was saved and incorporated into the new home was the front door, which was originally installed in 1930. The new home stands in the same spot as the original Follett House, though enlarged and modified. The new home included a two-car garage over which was added a full apartment. The living room was extended and the kitchen moved to the south side of the home. During the insulation installation they found the sheathing to be of 12-inch oak planks—no longer made. Many old features from the Follett House such as molding, doors, door frames, and door knobs were repurposed in the new home.

- The home is currently the private residence of William Dean Howells (W.D. Howells) and his family. He is the grandson of John Mead Howells.

THE HOOKE HOUSE
(A.K.A. ROGER RUSSELL/CAPTAIN HOOKE/MAYO HOUSE)

See Appendix I, Page 69.
Date built: 1674
Street Address: 40 Pepperrell Road, Kittery Point

Summary prior to 1947 as noted in Colonial Village *and other sources:*

This house was built around 1674. This area was later called Hooke's Cove. It has been under private ownership over the years.

After 1947 and current status:

- The home continues to stand in its original location. It is well maintained. Original features have been preserved.

- Following World War II, the house came under the ownership of Vice Admiral Morton Deyo, a decorated naval leader who played a key military role during World War II. Upon the death of Admiral Deyo in 1973, the home was transferred to other members of the Deyo family including his daughter Lila Deyo.

- In the 1990s the home changed owners.

- A key attribute of the home is its noted landscaping.

THE 1798 HOUSE

See Appendix I, Page 70. (*Figure 19*)
Date built: 1798
Street Address: 116 Pepperrell Road, Kittery Point

Summary prior to 1947 as noted in Colonial Village *and other sources:*

A well-known and admired home in Kittery Point is the 1798 House, as noted by a sign indicating the 1798 date attached to the outside of the home and easily seen from Pepperrell Road. It was built by Capt. John Moore of Portsmouth who sold it to Pelatiah Fernald, a sea captain. It is a one and one-half story home, which stood across the street from one owned by Pelatiah Fernald's brother, the preacher Elder Mark Fernald. The house stayed in the hands of the Fernalds until 1888, when the east half of the house was sold to the painter and author George Savary Wasson; he purchased the west half in 1893.

After 1947 and current status:

- This house, also referred to as the Pelatiah Fernald House, still stands in its original location.

- The home continues to be used as a private residence. Other than an attached greenhouse added in 1991, no significant external modifications have been made to it. There have been four owners from 1947 to the present. The most recent owners are Dean and Lauren Gallant who have owned and lived in the home since 2008.

- In *Colonial Village* it mentions the house was set up to accommodate two separate families. However, in recent years the house was arranged for just single-family living.

- Most internal features in the house are original including the floors and beams. In the 1960s the original plaster was taken down for electrical re-wiring. The walls were rebuilt with new plaster to look like the original. Later interior renovations have preserved or retained the spirit of original details.

- Regarding the '1798' sign on the house: It was carved by George Savary Wasson, who learned to carve from John Bellamy. It is likely 120 years old. On the advice of specialists in antique wood, the current owners, the Gallants, had an exact duplicate of the original carved by David Kaselauskas, from Kittery Point. That sign is the one now displayed outside, while the original is inside to preserve it.

THE 1763 HOUSE (A.K.A. FRIZZELL-PHILLIPS HOUSE)

See Appendix I, Page 70. (*Figure 20*)
Date built: 1763
Street Address: 154 Pepperrell Road, Kittery Point

Summary prior to 1947 as noted in Colonial Village *and other sources:*

This house is called the 1763 House, as it was built in that year by Andrew Phillips. Phillips was a descendant of William Pepperrell and was a Sergeant in the Revolutionary War. Over the years it has had many owners including Roger Dearing (also spelled Deering), Capt. Thomas and Mary Frizzell, and Roger Dearing II. It was in the family of Captain Thomas Phillips and his descendants for many years.

After 1947 and current status:

- The home still stands in its original location, adjacent to Pepperrell Road, Route 103.
- The current owners are Matt and Camille Brady.
- An addition was put on sometime in the early 1980s. The addition is L-shaped and extends off the east end of the house and heads south away from the street.
- The Bradys renovated the kitchen and turned it back into a tavern. During this renovation they exposed some old features of the home and reproduced others.

THE KERSWELL ORDINARY

See Appendix I, Page 70. (*Figure 21*)
Date built: c. 1720
Street Address: 2 Foyes Lane, Kittery Point

Summary prior to 1947 as noted in Colonial Village *and other sources:*

An early deed indicates this home was sold by James Kerswell in 1784. He kept an ordinary in the building. An ordinary is an early name for a pub where food and drink were served.

After 1947 and current status:

- This home remains in its original location and has seen little change over the past 300 years. The current owner is Trisha Olmstead, who has owned the home for the past 24 years. She recently had a historical search done on the home and discovered it was built around the year 1720.

- It has been used as a single-family home from the beginning. Deeds indicate it has had 15 different owners over its lifetime. Seven of these owners were from 1947 to the present.

- Many original features are still in the house including its beams and old wood paneling. There is a set of narrow stairs leading up to a small second floor.

- There is evidence of a past fire in the home with a few charred sections of some beams near the main fireplace. The date of the fire is unknown.

- The stone foundation and cellar remain much unchanged from when the home was built.

THE 1740 HOUSE

See Appendix I, Page 70.
Date built: 1740
Street Address: 74 Chauncey Creek Road, Kittery Point

Summary prior to 1947 as noted in Colonial Village *and other sources:*

This home, overlooking Chauncey Creek and Gerrish Island, was the home of Capt. Samuel Mitchell, a shipwright in Kittery. Only the core of the house dates from 1740; the larger part was built by the Amee family, who owned it for some time.

After 1947 and current status:

- The home is in its original location and stands today on the shore of Chauncey Creek.

- It has remained as a private home over the years.

- A historic marker was added to the front of the house indicating, "1740–Mitchell Amee House"

- The last addition to the house was constructed in 1956.

- The current owners have owned the house since 1998. When they purchased it, the house was not in good shape. Over the years they have done major renovations and restorations including taking the walls and ceilings back and restoring as original. The home's white pine floors and fireplaces were kept. During the renovations they discovered a secret room in the attic, which they speculate may have been used for the Underground Railroad or perhaps a tavern.

CUTTS HOUSE

See Appendix I, Page 71. (*Figure 22)*
Date built: 1798
Street Address: 14 Thaxter Lane, Kittery Point

Summary prior to 1947 as noted in Colonial Village *and other sources:*

In 1773 a two-story home called the Cutts House was constructed on Cutts Island on a site where Capt. Francis Champernowne had once built another home. The Cutts House fell into disrepair and it was demolished in 1880, which is the year Celia Thaxter and her family purchased 186 acres of land on Cutts Island. The Thaxter family built a new home, called Champernowne Farm, on the site of the old Cutts House, using original timbers from the demolished house. Soon thereafter, Celia Thaxter moved back to her home on Appledore Island at the Isles of Shoals. Her son John and his wife, Mary, lived at the Champernowne Farm throughout the rest of their lives. John and Mary Thaxter had one daughter, Rosamond Thaxter, who lived in the home with her parents. John Thaxter died in 1929; Mary Thaxter died in 1951. Rosamond was an only child who never married.

After 1947 and current status:

• Rosamond Thaxter continued to live at the Champernowne Farm her entire life until her death in 1989. Following her death, the house was sold and continues to exist under private ownership to the present day. Much of the remaining Thaxter property was preserved under ownership of the US Fish and Wildlife Service and Kittery Land Trust.

GERRISH HOUSE

See Appendix I, Page 73.
Date built: c. 1710
General Location: Kittery Point
Street Address: 70 Goodwin Road, Kittery Point

Summary prior to 1947 as noted in Colonial Village *and other sources:*

Timothy Gerrish (1674-1755) married Sara Eliot of New Castle, NH in the late 1600s. In the early 1700s they built a two-story home, named the Gerrish House, on Gerrish island fronting the ocean. It was magnificently paneled and was a fine home. Following their deaths, the home and some of the property was passed down to subsequent generations of the Gerrish family. One of the Gerrish descendants was Annie Thompson Gerrish who married Samuel Goodwin in 1791. Their son, Joseph Gerrish Goodwin, and his wife, Frances, had nine children, one of whom was William Hobbs Goodwin, born in 1822. Later in the 1800s, William H. Goodwin would become president of the Eliot National Bank in Boston as well as a Massachusetts State Senator. In 1882 he would return to his family roots on Gerrish Island where he bought 460 acres of land on the island. Goodwin tore down the old Gerrish House and built a fine, two-story home in the same location. The home and surrounding property would become known as the "Goodwin Farm" while the home was known as the "Goodwin House." Goodwin was well-liked and respected by the citizens of Kittery Point. He was generous with financial assistance to Kittery by improving the Gerrish Island roads and by paying for a new iron bridge going over to the island from Chauncey Creek Road. He would spend the next 15 summers at his island home until his untimely death in May 1897 when he was struck on the head by a falling tree limb near his home in Jamaica Plain, a Boston neighborhood. Following his death, his wife, Mary, would continue to spend summer months in the home until her death in 1910. The Goodwin family continued to frequent the home during the summer months until 1943 when the property was divided into small- to medium-sized parcels and sold.

After 1947 and current status:

• The Goodwin House still exists today and is located on Gerrish Island at 70 Goodwin Road, the street bearing William H. Goodwin's name. The home has 12 rooms including four bedrooms with their own fireplaces, and a large wrap-around porch. It is located on a three-acre oceanfront lot.

- From 1944 to 1963 the home and property were owned by Mr. and Mrs. Kenneth Archibald, where they raised their family. The Archibald family undertook the projects of upgrading the home's electrical and plumbing utilities. Mr. Archibald died unexpectedly in 1960, which necessitated his wife, Marjorie, selling the property in 1963.

- Ownership of the home then changed hands to a Portsmouth physician, Dr. Peter Czachor, his wife, Florence, and their family. The Czachors owned the home for the next 40 years.

- From 2007 to the present, the home has been under private ownership. Extensive renovations have been done throughout the house including remodeling the kitchen, repairing porches, installing a few solar panels, and replacing the exterior vinyl siding with wood siding. All repairs were done to restore the home to its original splendor.

- None of the Goodwin property on the island from the late 1800s remains in the Goodwin name except a small burial lot, the Gerrish-Goodwin Cemetery, which is located near the old Goodwin House. The cemetery contains the remains of Timothy Gerrish, his wife, and several members of the Goodwin family, including William H. Goodwin and his wife, Mary.

WHIPPLE GARRISON

See Appendix II, Page 74.
Date built: c. 1665 (c. 1660)
Street Address: 88 Whipple Road, Kittery

Summary prior to 1947 as noted in Colonial Village *and other sources:*

Built by Robert Cutt, this property was designated a garrison at the time of the Indian raids. It is the birthplace of William Whipple, sea captain and signer of the Declaration of Independence. It is located near Locke's Cove on Whipple Road. The most well-known Kittery family to own the home was the Philbrick family, which had ownership from 1830 to 1937. Around the 1840s, then-owner Jesse Philbrick "modernized" the house including the removal of its center chimney structure and the addition of two other chimneys used for coal-burning stoves. It is believed Philbrick also added the main wing, which connects the main section of the house to the garage.

After 1947 and current status:

- Today the house still stands in its original location.

- As mentioned in *Colonial Village* the house dates to c. 1665. Recent estimates establish the date as c. 1660. It is one of the oldest homes in the State of Maine and possibly the oldest Garrison House in Maine.

- It continues in use as a private residence.

- In the 1980s the then owners refashioned the interior into a 1980s-style.

- In 2017 it was purchased by its current owner, Michael Sullivan. Sullivan set out with a project of major renovations and upgrades to the exterior and interior of the home, while retaining the base structure and style of the original house. Interior walls were installed. Bow windows were added looking out over the harbor and dock. The barn was modified as a two-bay garage that is connected to the main house. Exterior painting and needed repairs were completed.

WILLOWBANK

See Appendix II, Page 76. (*Figure 23*)
Date built: 1727
Street Address: 124 Whipple Road, Kittery

Summary prior to 1947 as noted in Colonial Village *and other sources:*

   This estate on Whipple Road, the "Intervene," was built before 1735 and has been occupied by many familiar local families, with some family members buried on the property. In 1931, the estate was owned by John P. Benson, an outstanding American artist and mural painter, whose studio stood on the other side of the street.

After 1947 and current status:

- Today the house still stands as a distinctive and familiar residence clearly seen by those traveling on Route 103, Whipple Road. Over the past years the house has been well maintained. No major changes have been made to the original home in recent years.

- It continues in its use as a private residence. Its current owner is Duncan McEachern, a well-known local attorney.

- Ann Catherine Tredick Wendell, who was born at Willowbank, married into British nobility. The family's estate was Highclere Castle, which later achieved international fame as the main location for the historical drama series *Downton Abbey*.

FERNALD HOUSE

See Appendix II, Page 75.
Date built: c. 1690
Street Address: 34 Williams Avenue, Kittery

Summary prior to 1947 as noted in Colonial Village *and other sources:*

Built in 1690 at the head of Williams Avenue, this house faces the river has had several sections added to the original home. It was the home of the Fernald family for many generations.

After 1947 and current status:

• The home still stands in its original location.

• The home retains its wide pine floor boards, large locks, fireplaces with Dutch ovens, and a winding staircase.

• Over the years it has been under private ownership.

BADGER HOUSE

See Appendix II, Page 76. (*Figure 24)*
Date built: c. 1790
Street Address: 45 Government Street, Kittery

Summary prior to 1947 as noted in Colonial Village *and other sources:*

Though dated 1790, part of this house is said to be much older. The main part of the house was built by Samuel Badger in 1824. Badger built many ships in his nearby shipyard. The house, located on Government Street, faces the river. Samuel Badger was a nephew of William Badger who was also a shipbuilder and after whom Badger's Island was named. Upon William Badger's death in 1830, Samuel Badger took over shipbuilding at his uncle's Badger's Island shipyard until his own death in 1857.

After 1947 and current status:

• The home still stands and was expanded and converted into four individual condominium units that retain some original features such as wide pine floors and antique beams.

• The family burial plot for Samuel Badger is in the rear of 16 Otis Avenue, located near his home on Government Street. A distinctive monument for him was installed in this family cemetery in 1858. The monument was entered into the National Register of Historic Places in 1998.

RICE HOUSE

See Appendix II, Page 77.
Date built: c. 1750
Street Address: 2 Rice Avenue, Kittery

Summary prior to 1947 as noted in Colonial Village *and other sources:*

Built about 1750 on the corner of Rice Avenue and Government Street, this was the home of Samuel Rice. He was half owner of the ferry to Portsmouth, which was the primary means to cross the Piscataqua River between Portsmouth and Kittery until the river's first bridge was constructed in 1822. The Rice family also operated a tavern at the foot of Rice Avenue next to the ferry's river landing area. This tavern was built in 1777 and was torn down around 1940 after many years of use as private residence after the ferry was discontinued.

After 1947 and current status:

- The Rice House no longer exists.
- The home remained in private ownership into the 21st century. The building became quite deteriorated and was condemned in 2015.
- The lot was then sold, the house torn down, and a new building constructed in 2017 on the site. The new building consists of two individual condominium units.

DENNETT HOUSE (A.K.A. "DENNETT GARRISON")

See Appendix II, Page 78. (*Figures 25 and 26)*
Date built: c. 1710
Street Address: 100 Dennett Road, Kittery

Summary prior to 1947 as noted in Colonial Village *and other sources:*

Built in 1707, this house was designated a garrison in 1720 and is one of the oldest surviving buildings in Maine. Over the years the Dennetts provided local leadership and officers to the Navy and merchant shipping.

After 1947 and current status:

- The house is still standing as a private residence and is well maintained. It retains many original features.
- It continues under ownership of the Dennett family.

- It was listed on the National Register of Historic Places in 1978. In the application it notes this house is considered "Kittery's most completely preserved garrison house."

SHAPLEIGH HOUSE

See Appendix II, Page 79. (*Figure 27*)
Date built: c. 1735
Street Address: Manson Road, Kittery

Summary prior to 1947 as noted in Colonial Village and other sources:

Located across from the Shapleigh School in North Kittery, the house was built by Captain John Shapleigh, the great-grandson of Kittery Point's first settler. Captain Shapleigh was a well-to-do farmer and captain of the local militia. The last occupant of the house, Charles F. Shapleigh, died in 1906. For many years the property was held by a large number of heirs, so it was neglected.

After 1947 and current status:

- The house no longer exists.
- At the time *Colonial Village* was published in 1947 this home was in an advanced state of disrepair. The home was torn down sometime in the early- to mid-1950s.
- Today only a cellar hole exists where the house once stood.

DODOVAH CURTIS HOUSE

See Appendix II, Page 80. (*Figure 28*)
Date built: before 1700
Street Address: 435 US Route 1, Kittery

Summary prior to 1947 as noted in Colonial Village *and other sources:*

This house was originally located near Spruce Creek on Litchfield Road, which connected Picott Road and King's Highway, today's Route 1. It was built before 1700 and once was a stagecoach inn. It was the home of Madam Wood, Maine's first novelist. It was moved in the late 1800s to a new location on the Post Road (Route 1) across from Litchfield Road.

After 1947 and current status:

- The house no longer exists.

- In the early 1980s expansion of the Kittery Mall retail stores was underway. At the time, the home was associated with Morgan Willis, an antique dealer and auctioneer. The house was located in the area of the planned Crate & Barrel Outlet. In order to make way for the new outlet, the house was put up for sale for $1.00 so long as the new owner would move the house off the property. It was purchased by Harrison Lemont, a local accountant. In 1984 he moved it, at a cost of $40,000, to an area just north of the Malls next door to his Pine Tree Store at 435 US Route 1. Mr. Lemont moved his accounting office into the house while renting the building's other available space.

- Harrison Lemont passed away in 2007 and his son, Kenneth Lemont, acquired ownership of the house and continued to rent space in the building for several years. Because of the very high cost of heating the house in the winter and the projected costly maintenance needed to update the house, Mr. Lemont scheduled the house for demolition in late 2015. Prior to demolition much of the interior woodwork was sold to an antique dealer in North Hampton, NH.

- Demolition was completed in early 2016 and a new office building was constructed on the site, completed in 2017.

DR. DANIEL PIERCE HOUSE

See Appendix II, Page 81.
Date built: 1763
Street Address: 22 Picott Road, Kittery

Summary prior to 1947 as noted in Colonial Village *and other sources:*

Located on Picott Road, near the head of Spruce Creek, this house was built in 1763 by Dr. Daniel Pierce (at times, spelled Peirce). He had an office and drug store in the front of the house.

After 1947 and current status:

- The house still stands in its original location.

- It has been used as a private residence over the years.

- In the early 1980s the owners expanded the home with a two-story addition in the rear.

- Mr. and Mrs. John Mason, Jr. owned the house for over 30 years from 1983 until their deaths in 2014 and 2017 respectively. Mr. Mason built two workshops in the barn that was on the property where he kept quite busy with the "endless repairs" of the home, which, by the way, was his joy and passion. The first renovation the Masons did after purchase was to the existing mudroom entrance to the house and to move the kitchen, thus opening the space to become a combined kitchen/sitting room. Other renovations over the years included the powder room downstairs, the middle bathroom upstairs, and the master bathroom upstairs. Many colonial details of the home, including its fireplace, remain to the present day.

- Wendy and Bill Hummel currently own the house. Wendy is a daughter of Mr. and Mrs. Mason. Another daughter, Leslie Mason and her husband David Kerr, live at the house part of the year. All members of the extended Mason family use the house throughout the year.

APPENDIX III SOURCES

This project was undertaken by Thomas Prince at the request of the Kittery Historical and Naval Museum in anticipation of the Museum republishing the book *Colonial Village*, written by John Eldridge Frost in 1947 as his master's thesis. Below are the primary sources of the research conducted from January 15, 2021 to March 15, 2021.

Internet

- Numerous Google searches—all subjects and associated material
- Cemetery records (Rice Cemetery, Gerrish-Goodwin Cemetery, Kittery Point Congregational Church Burial Ground, Pepperrell Family Plot, Badger Family Cemetery)
- Web pages for commercial/public properties including Fort McClary, Congregational Church, Pepperrell Cove properties, and Kittery Historical and Naval Museum
- National Register of Historic Places
- Portsmouth Atheneum—on-line photos and files
- Historic New England—on-line photos and files
- Google maps—visuals of associated colonial homes and structures including lot lines
- Google images—photos of properties, associated documents

Newspapers.com (subscription service for searching newspaper archives)

- Numerous searches and date ranges for subjects associated with this project
- With emphasis on Portsmouth Herald feature articles and general information
- Obituary records

Town of Kittery Vision Database

- All associated properties—including year built and property description

Douglas Armsden photos—several properties

Books

Colonial Village. John Frost, 1947. Primary source material.

Two If By Sea. Marian Craig, 2011. Story of Follett and Gerrish Families.

Old Kittery and Her Families. Everett S. Stackpole, 1903. Subjects searched via Internet.

Kittery Ancient and Modern. c. 1930. Both versions.

Kittery. Andrea F. Donahue, 2016.

Kittery Kaleidoscope. 1976.

Old Kittery: 300th Anniversary/1647-1947. 1947.

Attractive Buildings Along Shore. c. 1905. Section on Kittery Point.

Miscellaneous

- Map of Gerrish Island land ownership from c. 1895—Rice Public Library
- Personal trips around Kittery and Kittery Point to visually view the homes and structures that were included in this research project

Interviews

Interviews were held with several of the past and present day owners of the homes and structures covered under this research.

CPSIA information can be obtained
at www.ICGtesting.com
Printed in the USA
BVHW042220110921
616416BV00007B/199